EVENT MANAGER

Over More Than Twenty Years of Successful Meetings, Some Tips to Learn the Convention Management in Five Days.

Daniela Liccardo

© Copyright 2020—All Rights Reserved

The content contained within this book may not be reproduced, duplicated, or transmitted without direct written permission from the author or the publisher.

Under no circumstances will any blame or legal responsibility be held against the publisher, or author, for any damages, reparation, or monetary loss due to the information contained within this book. Either directly or indirectly.

Legal Notice

This book is copyright protected. This book is only for personal use. You cannot amend, distribute, sell, use, quote, or paraphrase any part, or the content within this book, without the consent of the author or publisher.

Disclaimer Notice

Please note the information contained within this document is for educational and entertainment purposes only. All effort has been executed to present accurate, up-to-date, and reliable, complete information. No warranties of any kind are declared or implied. Readers acknowledge that the author is not engaging in the rendering of legal, financial, medical, or professional advice. The content within this book has been derived from various sources. Please consult a licensed professional before attempting any techniques outlined in this book.

By reading this document, the reader agrees that under no circumstances is the author responsible for any losses, direct or indirect, which are incurred as a result of the use of the information contained within this document, including, but not limited to—errors, omissions, or inaccuracies.

TABLE OF CONTENTS

INTRODUCTION 6

CHAPTER 1: CONVENTION MANAGEMENT 10

CHAPTER 2: THE CLIENT FORM 18

CHAPTER 3: THE PROPOSAL 58

CHAPTER 4: THE REQUEST 62

CHAPTER 5: THE ESTIMATE 80

CHAPTER 6 GUEST MANAGEMENT 96

CHAPTER 7: THE SPEAKERS AND/OR THE GUESTS 106

CHAPTER 8: THE ABSTRACT 118

CHAPTER 9: THE SPONSOR 124

CONCLUSION 136

ABOUT THE AUTHOR 138

INTRODUCTION

Sooner or later, everyone will have to face the organization of an event, perhaps small, but—in any case—without the right set of ideas and emotions, it can be incredibly overwhelming. But when you know exactly what you want to do, you can do it easily!

The organization of any type of event such as a wedding, a corporate event, an art exhibition, as well as a special children's party, is the mix of two different spheres of our life:

- **Emotional**—your nerves must always be under control, and your feelings must always be in love with what you are doing.

- **Technical or practical**—I mean, related to your competence or more precisely to the competence that you will acquire event after event. Because the event organization is a learning process that will last all your business life on. And it is **so exciting and so wonderful** because you never stop learning. Because each event is different from another. **Each one is unique.** Each one has got its special, wonderful, incredible sensation that you can feel only when you create an artwork or when you fall in love with someone. **And**

each event you organize must be your masterpiece. Each event will bring out all parts of you because you will express your creativity and your passion. You will create something from nothing. You will create something out of nothing, exactly how it happens when you fall in love with someone: **everything stems from an imperceptible feeling, an intuition, an idea.**

But, just as in love, the first feeling could become an illusion, and the wonderful wedding (not just as an event but—above all—as a marriage) could be turned into terrible trouble. Even your perfect event could be your most stressful situation in life for the huge amount of details, people, and suppliers that you have to coordinate in a perfect dance, where every single part has its role in perfect harmony with the other.

To make the event that you have in mind, despite the situations you will deal with, you will move all your nerves in the direction you have chosen, supporting your competence. **Strong determination** is absolutely important: it supports your capability and your will to move forward and find solutions when obstacles arise; because they will arise.

That said, we have just arrived at the book, with its practical tips to organize any type of event: a corporate meeting, an open house, an incentive trip, or maybe a wedding, a family day, or a trade show, etc.

The competences required are:

- Convention Management
- Guest Management

In particular, the whole set of services required for the realization of an event in every aspect could be distinguished in these four different sections, interconnected between them:

1. Elaboration of the Plan

- Searching for proposals for the identification of the most suitable venue.
- Elaboration of the actuation plan, the development of the most operational guidelines, and the evaluation of the estimated cost plan.
- Planning and research for sources of funding, involving both contacts with traditional customers and the agency's usual references and channels in addition to developing new contacts.

2. Communication and Public Relations Activity

- The management of relations with promoters and sponsors and with the authorities.
- The study and production of promotional material.
- The press office.

3. The Scientific Secretariat to Support the Development of the Conference Contents

- The management of relationships with speakers, the forwarding of invitation letters, the collection of their confirmations, the needs and requirements related to their attendance, etc.

4. The General Secretariat

- The organization and management of the participants and their accompanying persons in the conference regarding travel, accommodation, meals, on-site transfers, entertainment, and the social program.

- The technical-logistic coordination of the event through the selection of suppliers, the planning of the general and technical preparation of the conference venue, the search for translators, hostesses, and specialized personnel.

- The care and management of catering services.

- The administrative secretariat for the collection, accounting, and billing of registration fees, management of suppliers, drafting of contracts with sponsors, billing and collection of fees agreed with them, drafting of the financial plan, drafting of periodic financial statements, tax advice, the fulfillment of insurance procedures and legal obligations.

CHAPTER 1:

CONVENTION MANAGEMENT

The Convention Management is the way to focus on providing complete support in the development of events, tailored to the communication needs, strategies, and budgets as required by the customers, be they corporate or private. Sooner or later, everyone will plan some type of event. The event can be small or large, but no matter its size, or its target audience, every event will require a plan in order to be successful.

If the event is huge, let different people coordinate different activities, of course, under your supervision but working with a team is much more effective than doing everything by yourself: meet them to brainstorm about any problems that might arise.

But let's start step by step.

1. The Idea

From the beginning, an event takes shape first in your head, and then it becomes a reality. So, the first step is thinking about the result you want to achieve, looking for all the information necessary to make it happen: write all the ideas that you have in mind.

Write as much as possible, because it is important to not forget any details. This initial list will become the frame of your event.

It will be updated with all items as you accomplish them: the initial list indeed will go on and on until you get to the event!

2. The Proposal to Your Customer

When you have established what you want to do, you have to propose it to your client and—if they like it—you have to fix the date.

To ask for an offer (hotel, catering, seat, travel, technical equipment, bus, train, plane, etc.), you need a date.

Even if you have the best idea for your event, if you want to make it possible, check the availability of the seat, the availability of the rooms in the hotel, etc.

If you are sure that the location, the hotel, and the other suppliers that you need are available on the date you have chosen, then you can begin to work, and you can make an estimate to be proposed to your customer.

3. The Budget

If the customer likes your idea and approves your budget, during the months, the weeks, and the days before the event, very important is also thinking about what type of audience the event will have.

Mailing, advertising, press office, promotion: they depend on the kind of target you are going to refer to. The promotion must be tailored to the audience you want to inform and acquire.

So, after the logistic proposal and the approval of the estimate, it is necessary to think and establish a promotion plan, agreed with your customer, and—be careful—in the meanwhile, make sure to update any websites connected to the event.

Promotion is vital for the outcome of your event: an event without enough people or with too many people compared to the capacity of the venue is a disaster!

After these three first steps, you can start your operational work, but to perform it at its best, **it is very important to have a system or a method to organize your job**.

4. The Method

The organization of an event, in fact, entails the accumulation of receipts, as well as confirmations, invoices, and even general paperwork, billboard, or other forms of advertising, promotion, or mailing.

You must keep everything (also every email sent or received, every note, every type of documents) until the end of the event, because maybe, before the event, you could have the need to refer to them, but also after the event, in case of problems with agreements or payment by the customers or with the suppliers.

It is very important to save all the emails sent and received related to signed contracts, so **the more organized you are from the beginning, the better**.

5. The Services

At this point, you must think about all the services to be provided that have to be supplied under the very highest professional standards.

When you choose a supplier, for example, or a person for your staff, you must be sure about the quality of their job, knowing if they are a person that you can trust and if they have the right skills to do the job you are entrusting to them with.

Of course, the price is important: one supplier could offer a service at a cheaper cost than another, but if you choose to look only at a price, you will be wrong. Price is not the only term of comparison between two suppliers. The service that you require must be done in the best possible way, instead of being-full of mistakes.

For example, a poorly functioning catering can be seen not only by the approximate way of cooking but also by the presentation of the food or the way of serving the customers. The tablecloths are perhaps not ironed well, and folds can be seen everywhere. Waiters have food stains on their aprons. If they are not professionals, they do not know how to serve, and their plates or glasses fall off. The waiters' attitude may be rude or non-condescending, and customers may feel uncomfortable as well as eat badly.

The flowers on the buffet table or the centerpieces, if you choose an inadequate florist, could be dried or old or with colors not suitable for the customer's logo or tablecloths. The combinations are, in fact, very important. They determine a tone of color and uniformity in the environment, which must be in line with the overall style of the event.

Furthermore, if an event has a purely male audience, it is necessary to evaluate whether the centerpieces should be made with flowers or better to use pine cones, chestnuts, or other kinds of decorations.

And if the catering service takes place during the day instead of in the evening, the centerpieces are fine but without a candle. The candle is suitable for dinners but not always; it depends on the atmosphere you want to create. The same thing applies to other suppliers.

For example, a hotel may be a three-star hotel, but it must be clean and new. If the furniture is a bit old, if the toilets are full of silicone, or if there are holes or burns or stains on the carpet, the feeling you get is something dirty and ugly.

The hotel staff must be friendly, and the staff with whom you work for reservations must be available and prepared; otherwise, they will mistake the names of your guests and—when they check in—they will not find them on the list.

In fact, before the arrival of the guests, the list of names sent to the hotel must always be checked name by name with the reception to be sure that there are no errors. You can give the hotel a perfect list, but if the reception staff loses the room assignments or names, all your work is thrown away.

But let's take another example.

If you decide to print the menu or the program for the evening and choose a cheap or not very capable printer, just because it costs little, the result will be awful. Certainly, the color tone will be wrong, and the image will not be defined, the print test will have to be made and remade several times because it will be full of errors, and the quality of the paper will be poor.

Every product that you choose to create for an event, whether paper or visual, a catering service or hotel accommodation, must have a high, indeed very high, level.

The event is an exclusive product and must be organized with the utmost precision and the highest professionalism in all its aspects.

It is the end product of your organization, and it is your image that comes out.

It doesn't matter if the mistake is made by the catering or the printer because they are not very good, etc.: the signature, the brand that comes out on each event is always yours. So, whatever happens, attendees as guests and customers will blame you, as you are responsible for organizing that event.

For this reason, when choosing a supplier or hostess or anyone who will have to support you in organizing an event, it is very important not to base this choice only on the cost.

Similarly, when comparing the quotes of two suppliers, for example, who, despite having the same quality standard, have different prices, try to evaluate if you can get better treatment and why one costs more than the other.

6. The Choice

Leave nothing to chance.

Every choice made with love and attention produces an effect that creates value. **And the creation of value must be your final goal both in economic, social, and aesthetic terms.**

Your event must be beautiful, and it must be useful because it will make many people work, and it must be fruitful because it will increase the sales of your customers if their guests were treated like royalty.

A successful event is your success, and it depends on the suppliers and on the staff you have chosen: they can determine your greatness or your weakness.

This book can help you to find the right way to ask an offer to a supplier or to manage a customer, a guest, or a sponsor, but it cannot help you to choose a supplier or an assistant: it's up to you.

Do not be in a hurry. Try to think about what your client likes, but also what it is useful or not; what could be better for the event itself or not. You must lead your client, not the other way around. You must lead your suppliers, not the other way around. You must be the leader of your staff. Clients, suppliers, and staff have to trust you.

To reach this goal, you have to hold everyone in high regard: your customer is as important as your supplier and your staff because only working all together you can make an event.

Of course, a corporate meeting is very different from a private wedding or a children's party (although it could be very articulate on the occasion of an exceptional birthday or celebration). But each event has got the same frame. The rail or the route you have to follow is the same. The differences are only in the type of staff and suppliers you have to choose.

Said this, we just arrived at the second chapter that corresponds to the first step of your activity: **the client form.**

CHAPTER 2:

THE CLIENT FORM

The first operational step is the **client form**.

It is the method to collect all the suggestions about which we talked at the beginning of this book in a sort of a list, scheduled in an appropriate form: a minute-by-minute agenda for all the activities related to the event.

See it below and try it soon, filling the gaps with the appropriate description of all the things regarding the event that you want to organize.

You have to update the client form with all the changes and/or all the details accomplished during the whole period before the event.

Timing is also an integral part of the client form (look just below the example of client form), where all the listed activities are summarized in terms of when, where, who has to do them.

Client Form Example

Customer	
Title	
Date	
Place	
Official language	
Total participants	
Registration fee (if any)	
Patronage	
Treatment of speakers and guests	
Treatment of participants	
Graphic and printers	
Venue	
Technical equipment	
Catering	
Extra suppliers and staff	
Promotion	
Social program and gifts	

Timing

What	When	Who	Notes
Option on...	Expire date on...	CEO assistant	
Payment of...	On...	Videomaker	

Customer

In this section, you have to enter all the client's data such as telephone, email, mobile, address, name of company, administrative contact person, production contact person, marketing contact person, everyone's phone number, details for the route with GPS or navigator, other info about all the logistic, and operative and administrative details concerning the customer.

You can also insert here who is the assistant of, and if they are nice or not, or if they prefer a friendly contact or a formal one. All the info about your client must be entered in this section. It is a screening or an X-ray of your client. Every year, if you work again with the same client, the information in this section could remain the same or can be updated. It depends if changes occurred in the company or not. Also, enter your feelings about the client. I mean if you think they can have problems with payment or if they are a reliable company. Everything necessary to have expertise in your client.

Title

In this section, you must insert the title of the event and the subheading (if any).

Date

Here you must insert the date during which the event will take place.

Sometimes there could be an event that lasts a week (for example, a fair), or there could be an event of three days (or more), but on every single day, there is a different symposium, meeting, conference, trade show, or activity.

Everything must be detailed in this section. Date by date, relating to what will happen on that date. It is like a calendar with a scheduled plan for the things that will happen.

Place

In this section, you have to enter the name of the town where the event will take place.

Of course, add all the specifications that you need, for example, if it is abroad, if there are some critical things about the motorways or the streets to reach the town or if it is too far away from the nearest airport or from the nearest train station or other information that you think could be useful.

Write here also if there are problems with the council, for example, in case you have to ask for permission or license to carry out some activities that are not allowed in the town.

Official Language

In this section, you have to enter the languages that will be used at the event. If there will be one or two or more, you have to specify everything.

It is useless to say that if you do not speak all the languages, your staff must be able to do that; otherwise, you need hostesses and interpreter in the required languages.

You have to know at least one foreign language, and knowing a foreign language means you have to talk and to listen to it/understand it at a very good level. You must be able to manage all types of content regarding general information and your activity.

Of course, you don't need to know any scientific or commercial terms or words regarding the content of the conference, because you are not and you will not be an interpreter or a translator. **But if the level of your foreign language is low, please immediately attend a language course.**

You need to talk fluently at least one foreign language or two (this is better, of course). And also the hostesses: they have to talk at least one foreign language fluently. For translation or simultaneous, you will take interpreters or translators.

Finally, another important consideration about the official language is that all the communication before the event—not only during it—must be in the language required by the client: official text, email, letter of invitation, or subscription. The list could be long.

It means that the staff working permanently in your office has to be able to manage very well the official language of the event; otherwise, you must send each text to a translator—before making it available—and it takes a long time, over an enormous amount of costs!

Total Participants

In this section, you have to insert the number of participants who will attend the event, but you also have to distinguish the number of people who will take part in one or another activity, because maybe not everyone participates in the same conference, symposium, or session.

Some people, for example, can attend a sponsor's symposium, some others a scientific session or only the main one; the accompanying persons usually only participate in the social program and not at the meeting (surely they prefer a visit to the city center or to go shopping) while the partner is at work.

It means that in some moments/situations of the day, you have a total number of people altogether, but in other moments/situations, you have a lot of small groups, and each group does different activities.

It is likely that the different groups will have lunch or dinner together or a coffee break (usually the meals are together during an event) and/whereas during the scientific sessions, they could be divided.

The number is very important and knowing it in advance, before the event starts, is crucial. For example, if you have a meeting room for forty people but there are fifty participants, what are you going to do?

The guest management (described in chapters six, seven, and eight of this book) will help you to know in advance the exact number of people for each activity.

In each event, in fact, knowing in advance what every guest/participant does, where they will do, and when is the only way to reserve the right quantity of food, beverages, chairs, gifts, etc.

But knowing it first is also necessary to avoid a situation where there are too many participants compared to the capacity of the venue or, on the contrary, too few participants compared to the big dimension of the venue.

Facing a problem like a lack of seats or food or beverages is terrible, but also a meeting room larger than the one useful for the event is an awful sensation: it will seem empty.

In both cases, in fact, guests will feel uncomfortable, and speakers will think that congress was not successful.

The meeting rooms must have the right capacity for the right number of participants: not too big, not too small. The total number of participants that you write/note in this section has got, therefore, great importance.

The same applies to a restaurant room or to a location used for dinner. However, only in the case of a dinner (served at the table or buffet style with support tables), if the number of participants is slightly lower than expected, you can use trivial tricks to avoid bad feelings in your guest.

For example, when the people arrive, count them and before they take their seats if you see that the number of guests is lower than the chairs arranged, remove the extra ones.

Ask the waiters for help. The participants will be so busy in their talks that they will not realize what you are doing and, when everybody will be seated, the tables will seem full, even if one table will have ten people and another one only nine or eight.

The general feeling will be that dinner is perfect. This is to say that, if you know exactly how many people are expected at the dinner, you can manage any defections or a surplus.

And yes, because if you do not know in advance the right number of people, you risk placing more chairs than necessary, more tables and more food compared to what you really need. And you have to pay for everything you ordered, whether it is used or not.

For example, when you reserve catering for one hundred people, and they are ninety, it is ok: 10% more or less, it's not surprising.

But if you book the catering for one hundred people and they are only sixty, four tables will be completely empty and forty chairs too and, last but not least, you will have spent money on almost double the number of people who have eaten. It means that you do not have done any guest management or not in the correct way.

Usually, 10% or a maximum of 20% of people less than expected are normal. But more than this percentage is not good. It means that there was a mistake in guest management.

Of course, you can also have the opposite problem. For example, if you have reserved tables and chairs and catering for one hundred people and they are one hundred forty, what do you think to do?

It is a serious problem, because—on-site—you cannot have enough food and beverages, neither chairs nor tables for all of them.

Never put yourself in this condition. The total number of participants is crucial. And it is crucial not only for the venue, or for dinner but also for the other service, such as the hotel accommodation.

Try to think about the number of people who will sleep and when (I mean, you have to know their exact date of check-in and check-out).

If you book more rooms in the hotel than you need, you will pay a huge amount of money for nothing, and you will waste a huge amount of money that might be used for a lot of other things. But, if you book fewer rooms than you need, where will you host the people in surplus?

Maybe in the hotel reserved there are no other rooms available on the date you need (if you do not have reserved in advance).

You need to move the surplus to another hotel, maybe far away: during an important trade show or fair, for example, if you do not reserve the rooms one or two years before the event, you risk not find any room available on site.

In this case, you can find hotel accommodation out of town, but you need to arrange a private bus or transfer service to bring your guests to town every morning/afternoon (to go and return).

And also, in this case, the number of participants is very important. The private coaches/buses have different seating capacities: thirty seats or fifty seats or seventy seats (in case of double-decker) or similar.

The number of people who will have to use the bus service, of course, must be the same or less than the available seats on board: if you reserved a bus with fifty seats and you have to transfer sixty people, how could you do? Call a taxi? And where do you think to find an available taxi when a fair is on? It is quite impossible.

With correct guest management, you can know how many people will use the bus service.

And—taking a small margin—it is better to order a big bus rather than a small bus, because—unlike the conference or meeting room—people love to travel comfortably and if there are more seats than you need, it is better. People do not like feeling tight as sardines in a can.

This is the only case where it is better to reserve a big coach, even if the number of people is less than the available places on the bus. Moreover, the cost of a bus of thirty seats and a bus of fifty seats is not so different: so, if you have thirty people, reserve a coach of fifty seats.

Maybe, on-site, one more guest arrives; maybe the client wants to get on the bus with their guests. A few more seats are always better. And if there are people with luggage, a bigger bus is certainly more convenient.

Another significant situation where the number of people is very important to consider is the social program. For example, if you have reserved a tourist guide and they have to lead your participants or their accompanying persons on tour (maybe also a simple tour like a visit to the center of the town or to a museum, or if they go to a wine tasting, etc.), the legal authorization allows only a maximum number of people for each tourist guide.

If the number increases a little, there is no problem: you will pay the difference after the event on balance. But, if the number doubles, you need two tourist guides. And where do you find a tourist guide available on the spot?

Therefore, in this case, the guest management helps you to know in advance how many tourist guides you need based on the number of participants.

As you see, this section is strictly related to the three chapters of the book: number five, number six, and number seven. But this section is also related to the communication and advertising of the event. Even to the press office, sometimes. Why?

Because, for example, if your event is a concert or a political conference or something where everybody can go buying a ticket or even for free, the number of participants is guaranteed only by a good promotion.

Mailing, invitation, promotion, advertising, and press office; all these instruments are very useful for the success of the event but not all and not always you have to use them: it depends on the type of event you are organizing.

Needless to say, this also applies to those services for which you need professionals with a very high standard.

So, about the number of participants, you have to consider carefully all the factors mentioned above in order to enter the correct number in this section.

Registration Fee

Here you have to enter the fee that the participants have to pay when they register for the event.

Be careful: not all participants pay the same fee, and not all events require a fee. For example, if you organize a congress, usually there is a fee for participants and another fee for accompanying persons because they take part in different activities.

The accompanying persons, for instance, pay only for the social program or small activities together with the participants such as lunch, dinner, coffee break, or team building (if any).

The participants can choose if they want to register themselves for the whole congress or only for some sessions. The sessions can last one day or two days or only an afternoon or a morning.

The participants can also decide to take part in other additional activities such as a specific symposium or others to be described in this section, if any, with the correct fee. Of course, all this information depends on the type of event you are organizing.

Concert? Everyone pays, but the price might be different depending on where you sit, whether it is on the ground or in the gallery, or in the stands. Congress? Different fees for different activities. Convention? Nobody pays. It is a corporate meeting, and it is reserved only for staff, salesforce, customers, etc. Wedding? They are all guests.

This section of the client form must be completed considering the target or the audience or the type of invited persons/guests to whom the event is addressed.

Needless to say that if you are managing an event where you have to collect a registration fee, you need at least one person (or more than one, if the event is very big) to do this job. The time required for this activity is very long. The person in charge must be very meticulous. Better if they have administrative skills. For each fee, you must issue a receipt or an invoice.

If the event requires a registration fee, it means that part of the revenue comes from it, or all (rarely, but it could be).

Usually, there are sponsors or different business partners involved in an event where the registration fee is required, so the registration fee is only a small part of the amount of money that covers all the costs of the event.

In case of corporate event, wedding, or event reserved for guests only (celebration like the fifty years of a company or something like this), you must issue the invoice only to one customer (hoping they will pay by the due date, because you have to pay the suppliers and the staff, etc.). So the expiry dates of payment of the deposit indicated in the balance are very important to be respected by your client.

In the case of congresses or other events with a registration fee, the invoices to be issued are a lot: single participants, sponsors, scientific societies, etc. (it depends on all the involved subjects).

Anyway, if the registration it's a part of the revenue to cover the costs of the event, it is very important not to be wrong when you decide how much the registration fee must be. The decision must be taken together with the sponsors/clients/customers.

Pay attention: a wrong registration fee can cause a deficit in the event. If the registration fee is too high compared to the offer (the event itself), people can decide not to come. If the registration fee is too low, you will not have enough money to cover the expenses, and clients/sponsors/etc. have to pay the remaining, if they accept it or if it is in the contract that you signed. Be very careful with the proceeds of the event, or you risk losing a lot of money.

There is no event that costs little. So—if you do not want to organize it for charity—always keep in mind your budget and the related revenues, and especially if they come from registration fees—in part or entirely—please watch out!

It is true, however, that if the registration fee is correct and there are many more people than expected, your interests increase and therefore there is an excellent profit.

When you decide on a registration fee, you have to calculate the total cost of the event and divide it by the estimated number of participants you think will come.

Try to stay low in expectations, i.e., calculate a minimum number of paying participants, so—if they are more—your profit will be greater.

Obviously, if there are other revenues, such as fees paid by sponsors, then you will have to divide by the number of participants only the remaining part of the expense not covered by the sponsor.

Also, consider, but this is very clear and detailed in the chapter on the estimate that if you underestimate the possible unforeseen costs, though plausible, in the estimate, you risk not having the necessary coverage.

In fact, each event has an initial budget, which is based on minimum spending costs, but—in the final balance—the costs can double or remain very similar to the estimate, depending on the management of revenues and expenditures.

This means that if your client is not a company, and, therefore, if your event is not a meeting covered in expenses but a congress or an open doors event, you do not have a contact person to ask for the missing money.

Where do you think to find the missing money that did not come from the registration fee? The client company is, in fact, a guarantor, based on the contract you sign, of all the expenses that, authorized by the company itself (always in writing, never in words), you incur on its behalf. So, if the expenses increase, you are covered if the customer authorizes them. But, in the case of a congress, for example, if the costs increase and there are no other sponsors or other paying participants, who takes the risk?

This is why the registration fee is very important and, when you establish it, you must also consider the possible excess so you are more guaranteed. If the expenses remain contained, it means that you will have a higher profit margin.

So, in the case of a corporate event, you have fewer risks (if the company is solid and pays its bills), but you have fewer earnings.

In the case of a congress and an event with more payers (registration fees, sponsors, etc.), you have many more risks, but the profits can sometimes be very high if they could remain in your agency.

Oh yes, because if the agreement signed with your customer is not this, you must give this profit to them. So pay attention when you sign something: read very well!

Once the expenses are covered, in the final balance, if the agreement signed establishes that you and your customer will decide how to divide the additional incomes, you can keep them all or part of them, depending on the above-mentioned agreement.

But, if the money you earned exceeds the expenses incurred during a conference, it does not belong to your agency (unless the agreement provides for it). This money belongs to the customer (maybe it could be a scientific society, for example, in the case of a scientific congress), and it must be returned to it in the form of scholarships for trainees or by financing the research projects that follow, etc.

That is, it all depends on contractual agreements. It is clear that if there is a profit, your client is happy and will make you organize the next event.

So, pay attention to the registration fee you publish, considering all of the above.

Patronage

In this section, you have to insert the patronage that you have to ask for your client.

The patronage comes from a national or local council, an important scientific or political association, or from a theatre, etc. Patronage can be free of charge or for a fee.

Sometimes you have to pay for it and—even if it could seem a useless expense—some patronages are necessary to increase the number of people who will come to your event.

For this reason, it is better to make an investment which will bring you more money later rather than save money now.

Investing money in the right way with the rights people of staff and suppliers and with the right patronages is the best way to be successful because all this gives you the possibility to earn much more money from registration fees or from sponsors, etc.

Substantially, patronage is something that you will have to face in any event, which is not a private one. A corporate meeting very rarely needs patronage.

A congress (scientific or political) always needs patronage and not only one! There is no specific way or example of a letter to ask it.

It is a simple request, so you will not find any example of this in the book.

Treatment Speakers and/or Guests

Speakers and/or guests are very important for any type of event. They talk about topics relating to the event itself, or they are customers of your client, dealers, or wedding guests like relatives, friends, etc. In any case, they must feel pampered, well-received, treated like kings and queens.

The type and level of speakers at an event often determines not only the number of participants but also its importance (scientific, political, or commercial).

The speakers are always guests, and sometimes they are paid for their intervention/lectures/etc. In some cases, especially in the context of medical conferences, the speakers may also be surgeons operating live. In these cases, a direct video is organized with the operating room.

If instead they speak at the congress and simply project videos, photos, or texts, then their presence will be directly in the congress hall without external connections. Speakers are usually hosted both for their hotel accommodation and for their travel arrangements. Obviously, they need personalized pick up upon arrival and/or return. Moreover, if they must have/receive an attendance fee, it must be planned in the budget of the event.

Speakers often have exclusive conditions compared to the participants, also for lunch, which is reserved for them in a separate room or dinner, in a private location only for them.

This is not just for a matter of consideration towards them, but also as not to waste their time queuing at the buffet, as they always have little time.

Sometimes there are gifts for them, and they must be found in the room upon arrival, or they will be given directly during dinner by the president of the congress or by another person in charge.

As well as all the participants, at the reception, the speakers will receive the conference kit from the hostesses, but for them, at the time of registration, a small gift is usually added.

Speakers must be handled with great caution because they are often touchy or used to being treated like stars and, therefore, you must have a lot of consideration for their habits.

It is very important to have one or two hostesses in the plenary room available to speakers, in case they miss a pen, lose a PC key, need to make photocopies or others.

The speakers' table in the plenary hall, as well as in the rooms of the other sessions, if there are any, should always be set up with water, glasses, pens, block notes.

Next to the speakers' table, there must be the table of the plenary or of the room hostess or room hostesses, whose task is to change the name of the speaker on the displayer every time the new one climbs on the podium.

In this way, the participants will always know who is speaking, even if they don't know the face. Sometimes, in fact, many speakers are known for their names, but they are not like the actors that everyone also knows for their faces.

Obviously, their name is linked to books, research, their work activities, etc.

Compared to the speakers, guests can be famous people or simply important people for the sector to which that congress or meeting belongs.

Guests have the same treatment reserved for speakers in terms of hotel hospitality, travel, pick up, etc. Personal gifts and kits are provided for guests too, both at the reception and at the dinner.

As well as the speakers, they should be pampered and always made to feel the center of attention. They are almost always "first ladies" (just to say...).

In the case of a corporate event or a wedding, the guests are the participants themselves. Therefore, all participants are treated with the utmost care according to hotel hospitality and their travel, pick-up, or restaurant needs.

The guests of a corporate event can be the sales force as well as the client's customers. Clearly, in the second case, the treatment will be aimed at customer loyalty and, therefore, maybe something truly exclusive will be organized.

Depending on the budget made available by the company, the things that can be offered are endless: evenings in castles with gala dinners specially prepared, helicopter rides to get to the location, races with luxury or racing cars, etc.

The forms of entertainment for the evenings dedicated to customers can vary from classic to modern style and, in the same way, the activities which can be more or less exclusive depending on how much money you have available.

It may seem brutal to speak like this, but corporate can range from the most exclusive type, if the customer pays attention to quality, to the most miserable type, if the customer has no intention of investing.

Rather than having a large corporate event with many guests who will not remember anything good because the food was poor, the hotel dirty or small, etc., it is better to organize a small event but paying attention to every detail, refined, special, unique, tailored.

By behaving in this way, you stay within the budget agreed with your client, but you also remain in the hearts of those who attended the event who will talk about it so well as to advertise the company and be super faithful to it.

Obviously, if the guests are the employees of a company, perhaps on the occasion of a family day, therefore inevitably very numerous, it will not be possible to do exclusive things as for a few, but the attention and the quality must be the same. Employees, as well as partners, keep the company going and are therefore highly respected guests. If they feel pampered and well-received, their productivity will increase, and our customers will earn more and make more events.

So, we are all interconnected. The way we manage and treat guests is not just a job of the moment; it is—at the same time—the best investment that the agency is making in itself.

Treatment of Participants

The treatment of participants is established with the client. They decide what they want to offer to them. Hotel and travel arrangements? Only the event? Event and dinner? There are endless possibilities both for the event offered to the participants and for the social program related to the event.

For example, sometimes, you can have a team-building activity after the scientific session, and maybe not everyone wants to take part in it, so you must always have an alternative proposal ready.

Moreover, some people are vegetarian or celiac. Not everyone likes the same things. If you have enough budget, it is important to organize different situations/food and activities in order to satisfy each one or most of them.

And very important is your attention to children. If there are children at an event (corporate or wedding or other), you must consider what they like to do, what type of entertainment could be better, and what kind of food is best for their little palates.

Usually, catering for children must be specific. Children cannot have the same buffet as the adults nor the same beverages.

Graphic and Prints

In this section, you have to insert the references of the graphics consultant or designer or of the graphics and advertising agency that follows the stylistic image of the event.

If the event has many economic supporters, instead of a single graphic designer, we take a real agency that takes care of the style and image of the event from the invitation, the program, the menu to any other form of printed, billboard, or poster.

If it is a corporate event, it is generally not necessary to rely on an external graphics service because the customer has their internal graphics office. Or they already collaborate with a graphics and advertising agency, so they forward the contact to coordinate with. If instead, you need to organize a wedding or an event with a smaller budget, then a freelance graphic designer is a great choice.

The stylistic line of an event is very important. It is necessary to make it recognizable, to advertise it correctly, and to distinguish it from others.

Beautiful graphics immediately attract the attention of the public. Furthermore, the graphics, or rather the style established for an event, become like a logo that is specially coined and registered. It is therefore very important that each part that composes the event respects this style: for example, even the letters must be written on headed paper with the style and image of the event, as well as the mailings that are sent and that must contain that logo, that graphics, that style.

In some cases, it is possible to create a website specifically for the event or links or online tools for registering participants: these too (site, online tools, etc.) must always be personalized with the graphics of the event.

Needless to say, the choice of the image of an event and its style is very important: the elements on which it must be based can be multiple depending on the context in which you want to set the event, the message you want to convey, or the audience you want to attract.

If you use existing images or get inspiration from photos or paintings or from any other publication, you must pay copyright. Not everything can be used: you need to ask for the necessary authorizations.

Before you publish something that is inspired externally, you need to make sure it is not blocked by copyright or other rights. Once you have obtained the authorizations or rights to publish the image chosen for the event graphics, then you can proceed to create the various printed products or even the necessary signs.

In the case of advertising or print campaigns, you can buy pages in newspapers or magazines or on specific public suffixes. The graphics used in the advertising will therefore be reproduced on each object of the event, even the folder to give to the participants, the pen, the dinner menu, the personalization of the venue with any kind of set-ups, roll up, or billboards.

Sometimes some customers want the hostess uniforms as well as the waiters' clothing to be branded with the graphics of the event. And it is magnificent, in fact, to have a unique stylistic code, from beginning to end; this makes the event truly special and gives it uniqueness and identity.

Usually, the costs of the graphics consultant do not particularly affect the overall budget. But if instead of a graphics consultant or designer you work with a graphics and advertising agency, obviously the costs are very high, but this is due to the fact that the work offered by the agency is much wider and more articulated. Its work is not limited only to the graphic style but ranges over the entire promotional part and the activities related to it.

Venue

In this section, you have to enter all the information regarding the chosen venue. When you choose the location where you want to organize your event, try to think about all the things, the persons, and the services (overall information) that you need and write them in the client form, because when you are at the event, when you are on-site, you do not have time to get what you need, if you do not have prepared before the event.

The only thing that you have to do during the event is enjoying the wonderful work you have done, and the others will enjoy it with you. Site selection is very important; this is the reason because you have to set everything up. Inside and outside.

For example, do you need welcome banners or other information in front of the venue? When your guests arrive, they do not have to wander through a labyrinth, but they need signs. Make a reception and registration desk. They must be arranged in a way that—when guests are in the venue—they can see exactly where they have to go, what they have to do instead of wander around. The location must be accessible (better if it is located along major routes; otherwise, you have to provide shuttle services from/to airports and from train terminals or hotels). The venue must be easy to find and located in an area capable of fulfilling the requirements of clients, participants, speakers, etc.

If you have to organize an outdoor event, please always check that it could also be a covered place to go in case of rain or bad weather. The site chosen is one of the keys to making a successful event.

Do not underestimate any problem such as enough electricity, situation of the bathrooms, and other amenities.

For example, some venues have the ability to emit a propitious atmosphere to make the event successful, as a relaxed and comfortable environment: the background of the event is often provided by the event venue itself, and this favorable atmosphere is reflected in the guests.

Take into account several factors concerning the location. For example, when the guests arrive, will parking be a simple issue or an inconvenience? How far is the venue from the hotel, from the evening location, from the destination of the guests?

In your thoughts also include the venue facilities such as a catering service, technical equipment, music, etc. Does the venue provide for them, or do you need external suppliers? Does the venue allow the use of your suppliers, or must you use its own suppliers? Is the location able to host all the guests attending the event? The venue should comfortably accommodate your guests without giving the feeling of crowding.

On the contrary, they don't even have to feel lost in a vast oversized space. Remember to offer guests quick access to meeting rooms, slide center (if any), offices, reception, meals area.

Maybe, if there is a church too close to the venue, a loud and noisy concert is not suggested to be organized there. But also a corporate event, if it is too big with a lot of cars or lorries, can create problems in an area too close or just in front of a holy place.

It is very important to verify if there is a parking space or an area around the venue, where you can organize, for example, a show with fireworks in case you think to have this type of entertainment during your social program. This kind of show, in fact, could be dangerous. For this reason, if you do not calculate a specific distance from the buildings/palaces around, you risk causing a fire or hurting someone.

Finally, in this section of the client form, write even if the town is little or big or any particular details that you think could be useful. Maybe these details may seem silly or useless. In case you will delete them or will be information that you do not use: it is better to have more information than less because even all the small details could be important.

Technical Equipment

In this section, you have to enter the details of the technical equipment that you require.

Sound and visual service can contribute to creating an impressive, incredible, memorable event, spreading and enduring emotion of comfort, relaxation, or excitement.

This is the reason because you must pay attention to electrical outlets. They are essential for lighting, computers, and any type of technical equipment.

If there is a social program, maybe with a band or live music, for example, this entertainment requires a stage over the electrical outlets. Furthermore, caterers will also require a plug with a minimum of 16 amperes for the fridge, truck, etc.

Catering

In this section, you have to enter all the information regarding the catering that you have chosen.

Sometimes there are two or three different catering involved in an event because one is for the meeting venue, one for the evening location, another for a daily social program.

Write here the data and details of each one. After all the events, what people remember is—first of all—if the catering was good. If your guests eat very well, they will be happy, and your event will be a success.

People are willing to forgive a bad meeting but not bad catering. Catering is one of the most important choices when you plan an event. The typology of the menu, the quality, and service (high or low service) make the difference. How you behave with a person always makes a difference.

Each buffet or meal must include dietary alternatives because a lot of people are vegan or vegetarian; some can have diabetes problems, etc.

Usually, each catering provides dishes for a buffet, as well as beverages and devices for cooking and serving dishes.

The behavior of waiters and waitresses is also of fundamental importance. Everybody, you included, has to smile and be always polite.

When you ask for an offer to a catering service, there will be different menu options, and you will choose the one you think is the best.

Pay attention to the equipment such as plates, glasses, tableware, etc. Do not undervalue any details. You must consider everything carefully.

The catering must be able to provide food also for a small surplus of people who might arrive at the dinner even if they are not expected. The client can invite someone, and they can forget to tell you. Some guests can bring an unexpected accompanying person. This difference cannot be calculated before the event, but your catering must be prepared to face the surplus. Of course, in an agreed percentage (usually 10% or 20%).

Extra Suppliers and Staff

In this section, you have to enter all the services which can be required like extras such as flowers, photos, video, porters, security, etc.

The **decorations**, for example, will be different in any event: it depends on the arrangement you want to do. In the meeting room? In the evening location? Everywhere. It depends on the number of people, etc.

Decorations are important if you want to inspire a particular emotion or if you want to emphasize the importance of the event.

The decorations, of course, can also be sponsored banners, your banner, roll up, all things that you can use it for next year, and more.

The color must refer to the color of the customer or to the sponsor's brand, even if they are simple centerpieces.

Instead of **flowers,** you can use fruit or ribbon. If you do not want to give a sense of formality, fruits are better than flowers. Both have the necessary gracefulness to decorate beautiful buffet tables.

You can put banners on the tables, and you can also set up decorations at the entrance doors. Instead of a horrible panel, you can use plants to hide ugly walls or, if necessary, to separate one part of the room from another. Flowers and plants give elegance and enrich the environment.

When you choose a florist, they must be an experienced florist. Never be you to make decorations or floral arrangements. The floral arrangements can be rented. They do not last long, so—if your event takes more than one day—you need to change them every day or—at least—substitute the ones withered.

Most important to celebrate an event and also to keep a memory for you and your client are the **photos**!

The photos are important because, in the future, you can use them for event promotion. They are an archive of the events that have been realized. But they are also good gifts for guests: for example, portraits of attending guests in beautiful frames.

The price depends on the specific number of photoshoots and on how many days of work (one day, one evening, two days, etc.). For example, if the event is a road biker event and the photographer has to follow the participants, of course, the price is higher. In this case, in fact, you also have to consider meals and hotel arrangements for the photographer and, at least, for an assistant who has to drive the car to follow the participants running with their bikes.

In addition to photos, **videos** are also very useful. They can be a product that—specially structured—is used by the customer as a promotion, representing the most important moments of the event with their guests.

The video can be projected during the evening; it can have a commercial or emotional value. It depends on the goal you want to achieve.

The cost of a video operator depends—as the photographer—on how many days they have to work. It also depends on whether or not they need an assistant. If it is an event that takes place in a single location or multiple locations. If you need background music and, therefore, you have to pay and ask for copyright. Both the photographer and the video operator bring all the necessary equipment with them.

You must always rely on professionals because the level and quality of photos and videos are very important.

Before an event, it is necessary to make a briefing with the photographer and the video operator during which the customer also participates, so both can understand exactly the use of their product and therefore take photos and videos targeted for the purpose.

A wedding is not a corporate event, so the photos of the couple and their relatives certainly have no commercial value, as instead can be those of customers, guests, speakers. It is clear that, based on the type of event, the soundtrack that will be used in the video produced for the occasion will also be completely different.

The choice of images, colors, backgrounds: everything is made taking into consideration the type of event and the use of the video or photos after the event.

Among the extra suppliers, do not forget **parking attendants** (if the events are big, maybe you must expect a lot of cars and they could also be required) and **security.**

In each event, on the spot, there must be personnel in charge of the safety of all the participants who attend an event. Of course, security must also be ensured using monitors or other items.

Monitors can avoid troubles when at the event, there are celebrities or politicians. In case of a concert, security needs to be adequate: the number of personnel in charge of it must be proportionate to the crowded situations.

Adequate security, like adequate staffing, depends on the number of guests expected—for example, hostesses, technicians, interpreters.

At the door entrance of the venue, it is important to welcome the participants. If the event is a concert, you will need security. If the event is a congress or a corporate meeting, you will need **hostesses**. Every hostess must be very pretty, but also clever.

The hostesses are very important because they guarantee the progress of the event. They help to put people on the buses and count them, to be sure not to leave anyone on foot. They give information about work sessions and directions on where the meeting room, the toilet, the reception, the lunch area, etc., are located.

A well-prepared hostess can make a difference compared to a very beautiful one but unable to use the brain. Each hostess must speak at least one foreign language, must be polite, and must not chew chewing gum while working. The hostesses must always have the nail polish in order as well as the hair, absolutely clean and possibly tied.

They must have an elegant bearing. They don't have to be obsequious but always kind, and they do not have to wear high shoes, but with a correct heel, because they stand for many hours and their legs get tired. A hostess with tired legs will walk like a mannequin and will be ridiculous. They must have gentle makeup, and all must have the same color of lipstick.

In some events, in addition to the hostesses, models are also needed. They do not have to do anything that the hostesses do, but they only serve as image girls, so the clothing like the shoes depends on the situation in which they are required. Both the hostesses and the models must behave in a kind and correct way, no wink, no vulgarity, no attitude that can give rise to misunderstandings. They must follow to the letter the instructions given to them.

Both cannot be low in stature. Height is a basic requirement for both hostesses and models. Needless to say, the skin must also be luminous and cared for: there is no hostess with pimples, let alone a model.

If they had any, the make-up must be done artfully to cover any impurities, correct dark circles, make the face always sunny, rested, and bright.

On the contrary, the **internal agency staff**—for this reason, also must be polite, clean, etc.—does not have to be "a little flower" or have a certain height or weight. No matter the age: what matters is that they are a professional of the highest level, a person with solid nerves and great confidence.

The team you work with before, during, and after an event is essential: it must have great physical endurance because events often require exhausting hours and must never lose its temper not even when they are very tired.

For each event, you need a person in charge of:

- Sponsors
- Participants
- Guests and speakers
- Suppliers

On the day of the event, of course, you must arrive before everyone else, so you can check that all members of your staff and your suppliers are there. You have to check also that all electronic equipment is working well and that everything is arranged as you decided.

If something is not in order, only if you arrive before the others you will have the right time to solve any problems that can arise.

When the event starts, everything must be perfect. When the event starts, it is the time when you relax and see the "machine" works.

Each person must be briefed at least two days before the event. The brief must be precise and absolutely incisive. Your staff and your suppliers (**remember**) are your arms: if your mind thinks in a way and your arms move in another way, you are stuck!

Nobody has to do what they want if it is different from the agreements/briefing made together. Every person of your staff, such as every hostess or supplier, must do what you and them together had planned and agreed.

Your staff and your suppliers will be not only your arms but also your mouth: they will be your face (think at the hostesses at the reception, for example, when they welcome your client or the participants).

This is the reason because all must be like if we were one person: smiling, kind but professional and precise. They perfectly understood your briefing: you have to create a team, and a team exists when everybody keeps their individuality but in perfect harmony with the others. Each one must be able to support the others at any moment if needed. The same aim, same goal, same guidelines to reach them.

These tips are very important because the event is the combination of all these factors, and being united is the basis: everybody takes strength from the other and also joy. The work becomes funny, passionate, interesting if everybody does it in this way.

If everybody knows exactly what they have to do and knows what all the others (suppliers, staff, catering, hotel, etc.) will do, they will feel self-confident, and everything will be ok.

You have to create this situation with your team and with your suppliers before the event because—if not—you do not have time to do this on-site.

An event is a machine: every single part has to work in accordance with the others. And if you are able to do all these steps before the event, during it, everything will be so perfect that you will have nothing to do except verify that the «machine» works and that everything proceeds exactly as you planned. But be careful: never underestimate that something bad can always happen.

For example, some people could be late, or they could have lost their flight or the train. Some others could have a sudden illness or a heart attack during your event; an old man can fall down and get hurt, etc.

Everything can happen when you gather so many people in the same place and when you put together so many people at the same time. Anyway, and in any case, whatever happens: NO PANIC!

Following the steps of this book, you will always know what to do because you will always be prepared to face every situation and every challenge. Yes, challenge, because **the obstacles** (if any) **will become a challenge for you.** They will only be a little mountain to climb.

For this reason, you must be the first to set a good example: when you will be on-site, in any situation you will face, there will be no form that will help you but only your most important skill: STAY CALM.

The calmer you are, the better results you achieve and even your staff too.

Promotion

An effective advertising campaign ensures that your event is seen, read, perceived by as many people as possible. A good press office allows you to have the most important and most useful journalists for your event.

The promotion must be targeted or enlarged; it depends on the type of event you have to organize. If it is a closed event, such as a corporate event, in other words only by invitation, salesforce, or guest customers, the promotion must be managed through the guest management.

If instead, it is a concert or an event open to the general public, then advertising and the press office, but also billboards and other forms of information, are fundamental.

For example, a political event can be partially open to the general public and, therefore, may require a double form of promotion, that is, both the one aimed at guests and speakers and the one open to the general public.

In all cases, having a clear target of people to whom the event must refer allows you to choose the appropriate form of promotion.

Do not forget that promotion also involves web sites relating to the event and social media and that it could also include writing blogs. In other cases, it is very common to use email programs to send information to guests, in addition to the production of posters or brochures.

You can consider other promotional materials and not only those suggested here because all types of invitations are essential both when they are for everyone and when they are only for a specific number of people invited to attend. Usually, invitations are sent by email and/or by the envelopes by post (more rarely). The quality of the paper chosen, as well as the fonts, have a great impact on the people. Someone thinks that they can compromise or increase attendance. Invitations must be sent no later than three months before the event. Sometimes, more time is needed, and it depends on the type of promotion chosen for the event.

The invitations must include brochures, or program and a form for R.S.V.P. *(Répondez S'il Vous Plaît).*

In chapters five, six, and seven of this book, there are some examples of invitations to different types of guests/participants/speakers/sponsors. Here below there is a very useful form, to sum up, the mailing lists to which you have to send the invitations.

The Mailing List Sum Up

Name-List	Quantity (in the List)	Typology	Quantity in Delivery	Delivery	Total Costs
Total					

Social Program and Gifts

In this section, you have to insert the social program with reference to all the activities to entertain the participants. They can be team-building, dinner, excursions in town or in a wood (sports activities), a trip by quad. The list is endless.

The social program is the funniest part of an event. For example, if you organize a gala dinner, you must first be sure that the location is beautiful. This determines 50% of the success. Then that the catering is excellent: another 50%. The rest is an added value that determines your uniqueness: therefore, the floral arrangements, the reception staff, the parking attendants, etc.

Do not leave out any details. For example, a stage on which the event president must go up for the welcome speech or technical equipment such as sound system and lights on the stage: all these are essential things and must take into account the capacity of the room.

If you use the wrong sound system, anyone who sits at the end of the room hears nothing. Obviously, the room, as well as the stage, must be set up with the client's logo for the use of panels, banners, or posters.

If there is entertainment during the evening, you need to adapt both the stage and technical equipment to it. For example, if you have a band that plays live, you need some equipment and lights. But if you have a group of acrobats who must perform aerial performances rather than on the ground, you need adequate equipment.

If, on the other hand, you have itinerant wizards among the tables, caricaturists, or other forms of entertainment that do not imply particular arrangements, then the stage and technical equipment are only needed for the client and the presentations or speeches they intend to do.

If there are children in the evening, an animator or maybe more than one must be provided (it depends on the number of children). Even better is if you can also provide a makeup artist and—why not—a clown.

The menu must be chosen specifically for both adults and children, exactly as we have already said in the catering section. As you will remember, among adults, there may be vegetarians, vegans, or celiac; even children have their needs, and they must be taken into consideration.

If, as an alternative to a gala dinner or complementary to it, it can be the next day for an event that lasts several days, you want to organize a tour of the vineyards and a tasting of typical wines and cheeses, choose the best producer in the area.

The location must be very characteristic, possibly with historic barrels and courtyards or gardens that make it fascinating. There are cases where the social program is different for men and women, or simply, you have two different alternatives to be chosen.

This usually happens if it is a daytime social program. For example, if you organize a survival course such as a team-building activity and, in parallel, a historical-artistic visit to the city or a food and wine tour with final shopping, men will probably choose the course, and women will opt for the visit. But it is not said. There are women who prefer sport activities and men who love art.

In any type of social program, however, you have to think carefully about everything you need. For example, the type of clothing you need to recommend. If you need to provide special tools such as gym shoes or ropes (e.g., for the survival course).

You also need to think about the different course levels to offer, starting with the lowest. For the evenings, you must consider that the ladies, in particular, will have coats or shawls because perhaps they wear light clothes during dinner, but they must then cover themselves when they go outside. It is therefore always necessary to have a cloakroom equipped and with capable staff. The number of hangers, as well as the number of hostesses in the cloakroom, depends on the number of people attending the dinner or—in general—the event, and if it is a service that you have to take care of even during the daytime event.

People's transfers are also important. If everyone goes to dinner in their car, you must provide an adequate number of parking attendants and—above all—you must be sure that there is a parking lot that can contain the number of cars you expect.

If, on the other hand, private coaches are organized to pick up guests at the hotel, for example, and then bring them back at the end of the evening, you must be sure that the buses have the exact number of seats depending on your number of guests.

You must also have at least one hostess for each bus that takes care of counting people when they get on the bus and—on the return journey—takes care of counting them again, to be sure that no one is left on foot. In some cases, it may be useful to have a nominal list of those who use the private bus.

The hostesses who work in the evening must wear—as during the day—a uniform, but the evening one is different from day one.

Generally, a suit is most recommended. It can also be a long dress if it is a gala dinner. In this case, the shoes must have high heels. The care and attention to the image are fundamental to make any event elegant and are reflected in these little things.

The hostesses must also have the same color of nail polish and lipstick, both during the evening and in the daytime. The hair possibly tied, but not with the tail: if they wear a long dress, the hair must be gathered up like a queen. The same goes for agency staff. Suppose the sizes of personnel permit, clothing with a long dress and heels for the gala dinner is perfect. If the agency staff sizes are not suitable for a long dress, then the dress is fine.

For the hair, what is said for the hostesses is valid, but—if the staff of the agency does not wear the long dress—then the hair can be left loose, perhaps tied to the tail. That is, there is no need for a hairdresser like it is for hostesses.

There are many examples of daytime or evening social programs, as there are plenty of activities that can be organized to entertain people. For example, competitions with sports cars, a hot-air balloon ride, or even beach activities and cocktails by the pool. Obviously, what determines the choice of one social program instead of another is the budget. It all depends on how much the customer intends to invest in leisure activities.

Therefore, based on the social program chosen, you must evaluate all the suppliers and all the people you need to make it happen.

The social program, in fact, is an event within an event. Sometimes it's the most exciting part. Generally, if gifts are provided, they are distributed during the social program.

At the daytime reception, when the participants register themselves at the event, they are given a kit that contains a pen, a list of the activities with times and places, a writing pad, and brochures of various types related to the topics that will be treated during the congress/meetings in the various scientific and/or commercial sessions.

During the evening, however, there are real gifts. They can be of different types. If the guests who take part in the dinner are customers of your customers, you can think of making nominal plaques specially engraved with the logo of the company represented by the guest. Each plaque must be a unique job, so it is an expensive gift. Usually, it is cheaper but no less beautiful to customize an existing product.

For example, a bottle of wine or a shawl (to distinguish a gift suitable for men and one suitable for women). Choosing a gift is very important. For instance, on the occasion of family days, T-shirts can be produced for boys, balls for the little ones, flowers for ladies, and ties for men.

Obviously, all these products must be branded, which means they must be personalized with the customer's logo and possibly also with the colors of the company that commissioned the event.

In other cases, the gift may instead be the memory of the event itself and, therefore, as we have indicated in the section dedicated to the photos, a framed portrait. In this case, the gift will be sent after the event: this is a way to make a subsequent marketing action on the participants who—as soon as they receive the photo—remember the good time spent at the event.

But, if this portrait wants to be given on the spot, perhaps a caricature is more suitable than a portrait: today, there are the I-pad caricaturists who sketch the guest and send the drawing directly via email to their email address. Obviously, if the guest is pleased and gives their email address, otherwise, the caricaturist will make a traditional drawing on cardboard that can be given instantly.

Then there are important gifts that are dedicated only to a limited number of guests and which are not distributed to the evening or publicly; it could be the case of a decanter made by an important designer, etc.

On the other hand, there are minor gifts that are called "welcome gifts," and that is, those who are left in the hotel room to welcome the guest when they arrive. These are chocolates, flowers, or fruit but always with personalized container boxes with the customer's logo.

Together with the welcome gift in the hotel room, you must also put a welcome letter, which is a summary of the voucher (see the example in the following chapters). The welcome letter is used to welcome the guest but also, and above all, to remind them of all the meeting points: times, places, activities.

CHAPTER 3:

THE PROPOSAL

The second operational step is the **proposal.**

When your client form is perfectly filled in, you have all the elements at your disposal to elaborate a wonderful proposal for your client.

Here you will find the frontispiece containing the four main points in which it must be structured.

The proposal must be captivating, precise, short, and clear.

PROPOSAL FOR THE ORGANIZATION

of

NATIONAL CONFERENCE/CONGRESS/MEETING

Place

Month, day/s, year

- INTRODUCTION
- PRESENTATION OF THE PLAN

- DESCRIPTION OF THE EVENT (PROOF)
- SOLUTIONS SUGGESTED AND ESTIMATE

I cannot write here a complete proposal example because it depends on what you want to offer, what the client asks, if the locations required are available or not, etc. But I can suggest to you how to organize the content of your proposal:

1. In the **introduction,** you have to write the reasons: why you choose a location, a hotel, catering, etc.
2. In the **presentation of the plan,** you have to describe the event in detail, including the time of arrival of the guests, the beginning of the meeting/conference/wedding/etc. Of course, they will be only plausible, but they must be as real as possible.
3. In the **description of the event,** use the client form, and it will help you to write the text.
4. In the **solutions suggested and estimated,** you have to list the suppliers chosen, explaining what they will do and why, how you have done the estimate, and why.

Pay Attention

When you write a proposal, you have to think as if you were a participant, then as if you were a guest, then a client and, last but not least, you must think as if you were a supplier (otherwise you cannot understand the problems—if any—that your suppliers can afford, and you risk asking them for something not possible. If you are wrong in a requirement to a supplier, you risk ruining the event).

In other words, you have to put yourself in the shoes of everyone involved in the event that you are going to organize: the client, the participants, the guests, the speakers, the suppliers, etc.

Only in this way can you predict what will happen. A perfect event manager always knows what can happen or tries to know it as much as possible.

It does not mean having a crystal ball where you can see the future, but it means that with the appropriate instruments, you can prepare all things with the certainty that they will be exactly as you want.

In this way, you can avoid mistakes or reduce them at the minimum (if any). You are the intermediate between your client's dreams and reality. You can share their dreams, and you are the only one who can transform them into reality.

If your client's dreams are impossible, that is, incredibly high as a goal to achieve, then make them possible. Nothing is so complicated that it cannot be accomplished. There is always a solution to everything.

But—be careful—if your client's dreams are unreal, because they are based on things that are not achievable both for reasons of time and money, then you must guide them towards a correct path that allows them to realize the best possible event, but taking into account their initial plan/desire.

The proposal is the way to lead your client to the best event they can do. This is the reason because, if you follow the four bullet points above mentioned, you can elaborate on a perfect plan.

But remember that to process the fourth point (the estimate), first of all, you have to require an estimate from your suppliers, in order to see if the event is possible or not and—mostly—if the cost is accessible or not compared to the budget that your client has available.

In the next chapter, you will find some very useful examples of each type of request for the venue, the technical equipment, etc.

CHAPTER 4:

THE REQUEST

The third operational step is the **request.**

It is very important because if the request is exhaustive, your supplier will be guided, and they can be able to answer all your questions in a short time. If you are not precise, your supplier does not understand what you want and cannot reply appropriately.

To avoid submitting an email repeatedly to a supplier in order to get all the information you need, it is best to write the first request very carefully. Of course, if the event will be confirmed, the correspondence with the suppliers involved will be a lot.

Please, never throw away anything until the end of the event, and maybe not even a few months after the end of the event. Everything can be useful in case of conflict or if you have to sum up all the details in an agreement or in a contract.

Before signing a contract—both with the supplier and with the client—the correspondence could be important if there is something not clear or not well specified.

In the next pages, you will find examples of some basic but important requests, explained in all details.

- a. The venue
- b. The evening location
- c. The transfer
- d. The restaurant
- e. Catering
- f. The hotel
- g. The technical equipment

Example—Request of a Venue

Name of the event

Date

Place

To the kind attention of

Dear Mr. _____,

As Organizing Secretariat of the _____ on the subject, I ask You an option and an estimate about the use of the areas of _____, as follows:

- Preparation on _____ in the afternoon (from 2.00 p.m. to 7.00 p.m.).
- Conference _____ in the morning (from 8.00 a.m. to 2.00 p.m.).
- Disassembly on _____ at the end of the Conference.

List of the areas needed:

- 1 hall with a capacity of _____ persons (please specify which technical equipment are included in the costs of the areas hire).
- 1 hall for the gala dinner for about _____ pers. at 8.30 p.m.
- 1 hall for breakfast and coffee break.

- Area for secretary and reception point.
- Area for the stand (please specify the wideness—min and max—I can dispose of).
- Wardrobe (specify if it already exists an equipped point or if we have to fit out a hall sufficiently wide and whether You provide or not the staff).
- Possible parking area.

Added to what is mentioned above, I ask You also if You can give me the names of the referring persons whom You usually apply for what concerns the services herewith mentioned, and who among these furnishers are to be obligatory used if the Conference will take place by Your Venue.

- Catering service
- Technical equipment
- Preparation and advertising poster
- Florist
- Porter firm
- Transfer company (buses and private autos)

I will be grateful if You can send me an **estimate** about the costs of the above-mentioned spaces no later than _____, also specifying if the cleaning of the areas is included or not in the rent costs.

As soon as I receive this information, I will submit it to the customer and organize a possible investigation of the spot in time.

I need please also:

- YOUR CANCELLATION POLICY

- YOUR CONDITIONS OF PAYMENT

I will remain at Your disposal for any clarification.

Best regards,

For the Organizing Secretariat.

Example—Request of an Evening Location

Name of the event

Date

Place

To the kind attention of

Dear Mr. _____,

As Organizing Secretariat of the _____ in subject, I ask You **an option and an estimate** about the use of _____, as follows:

- Preparation _____ in the afternoon (from 2.00 p.m. to 7.00 p.m.).
- Gala dinner on _____ from 8.00 p.m. to 00.00 a.m.
- Disassembly at the end of the supper.

Furthermore, I ask You also if You can give me the names of the referring persons to whom You usually apply for what concerns the services herewith mentioned or any other information.

Finally, I would like to know which suppliers are obligatory if the Conference will take place by Your Venue.

- Catering service.
- Florist.
- Wardrobe.
- Possible parking (specify if present or absent).

I will be glad if You can send me an estimate about the costs of the spaces above-mentioned no later than _____, **also specifying if the cleaning of the areas is included or not in the rent cost**.

As soon as I receive this information, I will submit it to the customer, and I will give You my confirmation in time.

I need please also:

- YOUR CANCELLATION POLICY
- YOUR CONDITIONS OF PAYMENT

I will remain at Your disposal for any questions.

Best regards,

For the Organizing Secretariat.

Example—Request of a Transfer

Name of the event

Date

Place

To the kind attention of

Dear Mr. _____,

As Organizing Secretariat of the _____ on the subject, I ask You some information about the possible use of Your buses.

Transfer from _____ to _____ at _____ ca.

Transfer from _____ to _____ at _____ ca.

Informing You that for the Manifestation is foreseen the presence of about _____ participants, in addition to them there are also the accompanying persons that will take part in the program of visiting _____.

I kindly ask You an **estimate and an option** about the use of Your buses as follows:

a) Bus for about _____ (quantity) persons (to accompany the speakers and the President of the Conference, anticipating the transfer at _____ p.m. in order to avoid a possible overlap to that of the participants, that is at 2.30 p.m.) and _____ (quantity) buses for about _____ persons.

b) Bus for about _____ (quantity) persons (to accompany the speakers and the President of the Conference, anticipating the transfer at _____ p.m. in order to avoid a possible overlap to that of the participants, that is at 2.30 p.m.) and _____ (quantity) buses for about _____ persons.

c) Bus for about _____ (quantity) persons (to accompany the speakers and the President of the Conference, anticipating the transfer at _____ p.m. in order to avoid a possible overlap to that of the participants, that is at 2.30 p.m.) and _____ (quantity) buses for about _____ persons.

Furthermore, I kindly ask You some operative information, that is:

1) Is it possible to stop the bus for _____ persons in front of the Hotel so that the passengers can easily get on/off of it?

2) As regards the buses for _____ persons, is it possible to stop them in _____ square to make passengers get on/off of them? Or do You suggest another place?

3) In case particular permission for the stop is requested, can You assure me that You will provide for it?

4) On the bus's dashboard, we need to put a road sign useful for the passengers, with the title of the Conference. Will You provide for it?

5) In which place must the buses park at _____? Take into consideration the medium age of most of the participants; that's why we need a parking area as near as possible.

I will be grateful if You send me an **estimate** of the costs of the equipment above-mentioned no later than _____. As soon as I receive this information, I will submit it to the customer and organize a possible investigation of the spot in time.

I need please also:

- YOUR CANCELLATION POLICY
- YOUR CONDITIONS OF PAYMENT

I will remain at Your disposal for any clarification.

Best regards,

For the Organizing Secretariat.

Example—Request of a Restaurant

Name of the event

Date

Place

To the kind attention of

Dear Mr. _____,

As Organizing Secretariat of the event in subject, I ask You a **quotation** about a dinner in Your restaurant for _____ **people on** _____ **month** _____.

The people must sit in a **unique room** altogether.

The dinner must be **served at the table**.

The menu must be the same for all people.

The menu must include food (*num.* _____ courses, for example, *1 starter, 1 main course, and 1 dessert*) and drinks (*wine, water, 1 cup of coffee for each person*).

The cost of the menu must be per person.

The cost must include taxes and vat.

If not _____ PLEASE SPECIFY how much is vat, how much are the taxes.

I NEED PLEASE AN OPTION UNTIL _____ **date/day/month/year**.

Could You please hold the dinner in option until that date?

Within that date, I can confirm or cancel the dinner at all.

I need please also:

- YOUR CANCELLATION POLICY
- YOUR CONDITIONS OF PAYMENT

I will be grateful if You send me an estimate of the costs of the dinner above-mentioned as soon as possible.

I will remain at Your disposal for any clarification.

Best regards,

For the Organizing Secretariat.

Example—Request for Catering

Name of the event

Date

Place

To the kind attention of

Dear Mr. _____,

As Organizing Secretariat of the _____ on the subject, I ask You **an option and an estimate** of the following services:

- _____, preparation in the afternoon (from 2.00 p.m. to 7.00 p.m.), gala dinner at 8.30 p.m. (venue to be established: _____).
- 1 coffee break for _____ people during the Conference on _____ in the morning (at about 10.30/11.00 a.m.).
- 1 lunch for _____ people during the Conference _____ in the morning (at about 1.00/1.30 p.m.).
- Catering preparation in the Conference Venue (to be established: _____) to predispose in the afternoon on _____ and food delivery, early in the morning on _____.

In case the Venue will be in an Ancient Palace, it is not possible to use a gas-kitchen, but only electric ones, and it is requested an investigation on the spot in order to define which equipment to use (ovens, plates, etc.).

I will be grateful if you can send me an **estimate** about what above-mentioned within today; as soon as I receive this information, I will submit it to the customer, and I will give you my confirmation in time.

I need please also:

- YOUR CANCELLATION POLICY
- YOUR CONDITIONS OF PAYMENT

I will remain at your disposal for any question.

Best regards,

For the Organizing Secretariat.

Example—Request of a Hotel

Name of the event

Date

Place

To the kind attention of

Dear Mr. _____,

Please put an **option** for the longest period you can of the **following rooms:**

_____ SGL/DUS/DBL for speakers _____ (B/B)

In: _____, out: _____ (or some days before or after, depending on whether they are foreigner), at least one night each.

Rooming _____ days before the date, prior to your confirmation.

I would be grateful if you can send me an estimate, VAT, and city taxes included, if any.

I need please also:

- YOUR CANCELLATION POLICY
- YOUR CONDITIONS OF PAYMENT

I will remain at your disposal for any clarification.

Yours Sincerely,

For the Organizing Secretariat.

Example—Request for Technical Equipment

Name of the event

Date

Place

To the kind attention of

Dear Mr. _____,

As Organising Secretariat of the _____ on the subject, I ask you an option and an estimate about the following services:

Set up on _____ in the afternoon (from 2.00 p.m. to 7.00 p.m.).

Conference on _____ in the morning (from 8.00 a.m. to 2.00 p.m.).

Dismantling on _____ at the end of the conference.

Technical Equipment List

Amplification system with 3 wired microphones for the chair and 1 for the podium, speakers suitable for ____ cost _____.

Double projection screen cost _____.

Audio recording of the conference—audio cassettes on consumption cost _____.

Wireless microphones cost _____.

Double slide projections + laser arrow + cost overhead projector cost _____.

Video projection (standard VHS) + card and VGA cable for computer projection cost _____.

System with speaker recording and projection on screen cost _____.

Simultaneous translation facility (in plenary) cost _____.

Projectors for double and single slide projection cost _____.

Screens 180x180 cm^2 cost _____.

Telephone line connection (tel. + fax) cost _____.

Fax machine cost _____.

WIFI, etc.

I would be grateful if you could get me a quote relating to the cost of the above-mentioned equipment today.

As soon as I have this information, I will take care of submitting it to the customer and agreeing on a possible inspection as soon as possible.

I need please also:

- YOUR CANCELLATION POLICY.
- YOUR CONDITIONS OF PAYMENT.

Remaining available for any clarification, the opportunity is welcome to send my best regards.

For the Organizing Secretariat.

CHAPTER 5:

THE ESTIMATE

The estimate must be drawn on the basis of the information collected. It must be summarized by chapters, each indicated with a letter. Within each chapter, the items deemed necessary for the implementation of the project must be described.

In this list, you have to write also the cost that you think to have because there will be a lot of expenses in the upcoming days or months before an event: for example, hotel and travel arrangements, venue, food, technical equipment, social program, excursions, etc.

Usually, hotel and travel arrangements are the most considerable costs, in any event, so don't underestimate them. Then, food and social program: they can also be very high, and they depend on the event that you will do. Where available, the price of the individual item is quantified; otherwise, it is indicated as "bottom of," intended as the maximum amount that can be spent for that item, and that is adjusted to the actual expenditure in the final balance or during the work, where possible.

All items not requested by the customer at this stage but listed as possible alternatives to those present and/or additions are inserted between an asterisk and not added to the totals.

As regards the drafting of the revenue plan, the quotas proposed are based on the information received and on the quality and quantity of services that are intended to be offered. The fee applied as an organizational consultancy is either a percentage of the costs or fixed; this at the discretion of the event organizer.

The elaboration of an estimate takes one day if you have all the info you need from your client and all the offers from your suppliers.

The budget for an event is one of the most important aspects of a successful event. A lot of factors must be considered like deposits for venues, speakers refunds, deposit for hotel, catering, photographers, bands, audio-video, and sound equipment as well as contracting the services of writers, actors, the ticket for planes and trains, etc.

If advertising and promotion are part of the event, there will also be advanced payments for the newspaper, radio, and television advertising.

Other expenses to consider could be gifts, or professional decorators, or planners.

In the document below described, there are all the voices mentioned: you can cut off or keep all of them; it depends on the event you have to organize.

At the time of the assignment, an advance fund is required for the costs of starting the works.

Example—An Estimate

	DESCRIPTION	QUANTITY	TOTAL	SUM
A	TITLE			
	DATE	When		
	PLACE	Where		
	OFFICIAL LANGUAGE	Language		
	TOT. ESTIMATED PARTICIPANTS	Quantity		
B	TREATMENT SPEAKERS AND GUESTS			
Hotel accommodation				2
B1	Hotel ___ num. ___ rooms ___ num. ___ of nights.	SGL: €. ___ DUS: €. ___ TPL: €. ___	€…1,00	
B2	Hotel ___ num. ___ rooms ___ num. ___ of nights.	SGL: €. ___ DUS: €. ___ TPL: €. ___	€…1,00	
Travel arrangement and transfer				4
B3	Flight	Details of flight ticket and cost	€…1,00	
B4	Train	Details of train ticket and cost	€…1,00	
B5	Taxi		€…1,00	
B6	Reimbursement		€…1,00	
Speakers and guests management				1
B7	Drawing up of the inviting letters; recall for presence confirmation; possible text request; report title; logistic coordination of travel arrangements and hotel reservation	€. ___ each	€…1,00	

C	GRAFIC		
Only for D1–D4			2
C1	Definition of the Conference's graphic image	€…1,00	
C2	Proof-reading before the photocomposition (till 3 rounds) and after photocomposition (till 2 rounds) + typographical coordination	€…1,00	
From D5 on, except D9, D12, D24, D25			2
C3	Definition of the Conference's graphic image	€…1,00	
C4	Proof-reading before the photocomposition (till 3 rounds) and after photocomposition (till 2 rounds) + typographical coordination	€…1,00	
Graphic for D9, D12, D24, D25: to be quoted, if requested			
D	PRINTED		
Standard production			19
D1	Preliminary program 1st announcement: closed format _____, four-color, two-color, one-color, paper _____	n. __ x €. __ each	€…1,00
D2	Reply	n. __ x €. __ each	€…1,00
D3	Hotel reservation form	n. __ x €. __ each	€…1,00
D4	An envelope containing the program (both the preliminary and the 2nd announcement, if the production is established)	n. __ x €. __ each	€…1,00
D5	Brand	n. __ x €. __ each	€…1,00
D6	Headed paper (1st sheet)	n. __ x €. __ each	€…1,00
D7	Headed paper (2nd sheet)	n. __ x €. __ each	€…1,00

D8	Abstract form	n. __ x €. __ each	€...1,00
D9	Second program or pre-definitive program	n. __ x €. __ each	€...1,00
D10	Registration form ____	n. __ x €. __ each	€...1,00
D11	Hotel reservation form __ for the second program	n. __ x €. __ each	€...1,00
D12	Definitive program: format ____ (without a hotel reservation and registration forms)	n. __ x €. __ each	€...1,00
D13	A folder containing the presentation of the material to the sponsor: format ____ colors ____	n. __ x €. __ each	€...1,00
D14	An envelope containing folders for the sponsor material	n. __ x €. __ each	€...1,00
D15	Badge: one, two, or four colors	n. __ x €. __ each	€...1,00
D16	Certificates: one, two, or four colors	n. __ x €. __ each	€...1,00
D17	A folder containing congress material: format ____	n. __ x €. __ each	€...1,00
D18	Note-book: format ____, paper ____ gr., of 4-2-1 colors	n. __ x €. __ each	€...1,00
D19	Printing plants		€...1,00
Extra printed			5
D20	Evening invitation with coupled envelope: format ____	n. __ x €. __ each	€...1,00
D21	Breakfast invitation with coupled envelope: format	n. __ x €. __ each	€...1,00

D22	Hall program	n. __ x €. __ each	€...1,00	
D23	Menu	n. __ x €. __ each	€...1,00	
D24	Printing plants		€...1,00	
Additional printed				3
D25	Abstract book	n. __ x €. __ each	€...1,00	
D26	Proceedings book	n. __ x €. __ each	€...1,00	
D27	Printing plants		€...1,00	
Content processing				1
D28	€. __ for each program produced (included envelopes and forms, if any) + €. __ for each additional printed	Starting from	€...1,00	
N.B.	*Content processing for abstract book and/or proceedings book: to be quoted, if it is requested*			
E	**CONGRESS VENUE AND PREPARATION**			
Venue				6
E1	Rent space, days of preparation and dismantling included		€...1,00	
E2	Cleaning agency		€...1,00	
E3	Cloakroom (with or without staff)		€...1,00	
E4	Costs of the staff (extra hours or overseeing—depends on the venue)		€...1,00	
E5	Parking		€...1,00	
E6	Insurance or vigilance (if required by the venue)		€...1,00	
Set up				6
E7	Preparation of reception, meeting hall, and		€...1,00	

	press office with tables and sign			
E8	Hall advertising poster	n. __ x €. __ each	€...1,00	
E9	Entrance advertising poster	n. __ x €. __ each	€...1,00	
E10	Road sign	n. __ x €. __ each	€...1,00	
E11	Wall poster	n. __ x €. __ each	€...1,00	
E12	Place-mark for speakers on the president table	n. __ x €. __ each	€...1,00	
Set up and dismantling				1
E13	Set up, dismantling and transport and/or storage of goods (if any) and technical installation, etc.		€...1,00	
F	**VISUAL-SOUND SERVICES IN CONGRESS VENUE**			
Plenary room				9
F1	Amplification system with 3 cables microphones for the chairmanship and 1 for the podium, service audio suitable to space		€...1,00	
F2	Screen	n. __ x €. __ each	€...1,00	
F3	Tape-recording of the Conference	n. __ x €. __ each	€...1,00	
F4	Wireless microphone + one clip	n. __ x €. __ each	€...1,00	
F5	Slide projection	n. __ x €. __ each	€...1,00	
F6	Laser arrow	n. __ x €. __ each	€...1,00	
F7	Over-head projector	n. __ x €. __ each	€...1,00	
F8	Video projection + VGA cable for computer	n. __ x €. __ each	€...1,00	

	projection + pen drive			
F9	Cabin for a foreign language with ____ receivers	n. ___ x €. ___ each	€...1,00	
Slide center		n. ___ x €. ___ each		3
F10	Projectors for double or single slides	n. ___ x €. ___ each	€...1,00	
F11	Carousel	n. ___ x €. ___ each	€...1,00	
F12	Screen	n. ___ x €. ___ each	€...1,00	
Reception/press office/secretary office				5
F13	Computer in reception	n. ___ x €. ___ each	€...1,00	
F14	Printer (like ____) in reception	n. ___ x €. ___ each	€...1,00	
F15	The fax machine in reception	n. ___ x €. ___ each	€...1,00	
F16	Photocopy in reception	n. ___ x €. ___ each	€...1,00	
F17	Connection phone plus internet	n. ___ x €. ___ each	€...1,00	
Integrative proposals				5
F18	Speaker projection	n. ___ x €. ___ each	€...1,00	
F19	On-air/videoconference	n. ___ x €. ___ each	€...1,00	
F20	Rear projection	n. ___ x €. ___ each	€...1,00	
F21	Computer in plenary room	n. ___ x €. ___ each	€...1,00	
F22	Lighting system with technician included		€...1,00	
Set up and dismantling				1

F23	Set up and dismantling and transport and/or storage of goods (if any) and technical installation, etc.		€...1,00	
G	**RESTORATION IN CONGRESS VENUE**			
Day _____ start at 2.00 p.m.				2
G1	Welcome cocktail on _____	Num. __ welcome cocktail at € __ x tot __ people	€...1,00	
G2	Coffee break on _____	Num. __ welcome cocktail at € __ x tot __ people	€...1,00	
Day _____ start at _____				3
G3	Coffee break on ___	Num. __ welcome cocktail at € __ x tot __ people	€...1,00	
G4	Lunch on ___	Num. __ lunch at € __ x tot __ people	€...1,00	
G5	Farewell cocktail on ___ or dinner on ___ or gala dinner on ___	Num. __ farewell cocktail at € __ x tot __ people	€...1,00	
H	**DECORATIONS IN CONGRESS VENUE**			
Several things				4
H1	Flowers and plants	n. __ x €. __ each	€...1,00	

H2	Transport and porterage of the secretary's material from office to the congress venue and return		€...1,00	
H3	Photos and/or video		€...1,00	
H4	Fire extinguishers	n. __ x €. __ each	€...1,00	
I	**STAFF OF THE CONGRESS VENUE**			
Hostess				2
I1	Hostess (n. __ in the hall, n. __ at slide center, n. __ in reception, n. __ in wardrobe—if there's no local staff) for a total of __	n. __ x €. __ each	€...1,00	
I2	Uniforms, also the changes	n. __ x €. __ each	€...1,00	
Technicians				2
I3	Sound-visual technician plenary hall	n. __ x €. __ each	€...1,00	
I4	Hall-slide and PC technician	n. __ x €. __ each	€...1,00	
Else				1
I5	Interpreters and translators and/or tourist guides and/or ____. It depends on the event	n. __ x €. __ each	€...1,00	
L	**DAY-EVENING SOCIAL PROGRAM**			
Social daily program—days ___				9
L1	Program of visits to choose among the agreed localities **during the Conference** (only the accompanying persons); **post Conference** can take part participants and accompanying persons that	Town __ = €. __ each one	€...1,00	

	have previously required and reserved it			
L2	Hostess for welcome/meeting point for visits program	n. __ x €. __ each	€...1,00	
L3	Sign for meeting point	n. __ x €. __ each	€...1,00	
L4	Advertising posters on the bus dashboard to make them recognizable for participants, so they don't get on the wrong bus	n. __ x €. __ each	€...1,00	
L5	Entrance tickets for Museums/Companies mentioned in the program	n. __ x €. __ each	€...1,00	
L6	GT bus to reach the __ mentioned in the visit program	n. __ x €. __ each	€...1,00	
L7	Technician	n. __ x €. __ each	€...1,00	
L8	Insurance		€...1,00	
L9	Dinner in typical tavern/restaurant—drinks included		€...1,00	
Night–day ____ : hypothesis supper with the concert				10
L10	Villa __ Hall's __ capacity __ max, not more		€...1,00	
L11	Catering		€...1,00	
L12	Transfer to reach the villa	n. __ x €. __ each	€...1,00	
L13	Welcome hostess before, after, and during the evening	n. __ x €. __ each	€...1,00	
L14	Entertainment (music, classic music, operas, jazz band, rock, different performances)		€...1,00	

L15	Copyright		€...1,00	
L16	Decorations with flowers and plants	n. __ x €. __ each	€...1,00	
L17	Cloakroom (well supplied and with staff members)		€...1,00	
L18	Cleaning agency		€...1,00	
L19	Lamps, service audio, etc.		€...1,00	
M	**GENERAL SECRETARIAT**			
Expenses				13
M1	Programs sending 1st announcement to the mailing list	n. __ x €. __ each	€...1,00	
M2	Programs sending 2nd announcement to the mailing list	n. __ x €. __ each	€...1,00	
M3	Letters sending to speakers and guests with programs enclosed	n. __ x €. __ each	€...1,00	
M4	Letter sending to speakers and guests for logistic agreements/delivery travel tickets, hotel vouchers, else	n. __ x €. __ each	€...1,00	
M5	Invitations letters sending to the mailing list	n. __ x €. __ each	€...1,00	
M6	Forwarding by post or by express couriers useful during the process	n. __ x €. __ each	€...1,00	
M7	Parcels forwarding in __ (country)	n. __ x €. __ each	€...1,00	
M8	Parcels forwarding abroad	n. __ x €. __ each	€...1,00	
M9	Possible computer fingering of addresses and printing on labels and on the list	n. __ x €. __ each	€...1,00	

M10	Possible research of missing data	n. __ x €. __ each	€...1,00	
M11	Service of labeling, postage, and enveloping for num. ___. Envelopes num. ___ sending (1st and 2nd announcement + inviting letters)	n. __ x €. __ each	€...1,00	
M12	Folders preparation for the Conference	n. __ x €. __ each	€...1,00	
M13	Badge preparation (with laser printed name) for the Conference	n. __ x €. __ each	€...1,00	
N	**EXTRA COUNTABILTY SECRETARIAT**			
	Expenses			6
N1	Conference participants without registration-fee and list	n. __ x €. __ each	€...1,00	
N2	Conference participants with registration-fee and list	n. __ x €. __ each	€...1,00	
N3	Necessary revenue stamps	bottom of	€...1,00	
N4	Phone	bottom of	€...1,00	
N5	Fax e-mail	bottom of	€...1,00	
N6	Photocopies	bottom of	€...1,00	
O	**ADMINISTRATIVE SECRETARIAT**			
Forfait				3
O1	Receiving of the sums agreed with the sponsors and with the distributing structures by invoicing, the amount collected of the registration-fee of the participants with invoicing release and/or receipt depending on the participants' fiscal position			
O2	Management of the relationship with the suppliers included the payment dates of the advice and of the services received that will be directly invoiced to _____ (CUSTOMER—IF THEY DIRECTLY PAY THE SUPPLIERS) and settled by themselves at the end of the			

	manifestation, within thirty days from the invoicing date		
O3	Accountability by drawing up of the pre-final budget (____ days before the beginning of the manifestation) and final budget (at the end of the manifestation), of the amounts collected directly or indirectly by _____ (CUSTOMER—IF THEY PAY DIRECTLY THE SUPPLIERS) on the basis of the present budget		
P	**PRESS OFFICE AND BILL—POSTING**		
Press office			3
P1	Local (with press conference c/o customer offices or another venue, only if free)	€…1,00	
P2	Regional (with press conference c/o customer offices or another venue, only if free)	€…1,00	
P3	National (with press conference c/o customer offices or another venue, only if free)	€…1,00	
Bill-posting			3
P4	Local bill-posting of posters num. ___	€…1,00	
P5	Regional bill-posting of posters num. ___	€…1,00	
P6	National bill-posting of posters num. ___	€…1,00	
Q	**SEVERAL THINGS**		
Further details			2
Q1	Connection transfer guests from the hotel to the Congress venue	num. __ bus x __ people €. __each	€…1,00
Q2	Congress kit or gifts for speakers, etc.	num. ___ x num. ___ people €. ___ each	€…1,00
Q3	Hotel settling for the staff of the Organizing Secretariat and administration annexed to the Conference	on the balance	
Q4	Travels and transfer for the staff of the Organizing Secretariat annexed to the Conference	on the balance	
Q5	Chancellery included a monthly amount for	on the	

	ordinary chancellery; the necessary for congress (pens for participants, glue, etc.); n. ___ plastic bags frame, etc.	balance
Q6	Translation of texts (letters, contracts, etc.) or other several things	on the balance
R	**TOTAL POINTS FROM A TO Q**	
S	**AGENCY FEE**	
T	**SUM**	
U	**VAT (if any)**	
V	**GENERAL TOTAL WITH VAT INCLUDED**	

CHAPTER 6

GUEST MANAGEMENT

The Guest Management activity is structured by sending the invitation in PDF format (sent by the event agency or directly by the client according to the company policy).

There are many shipments during the months leading up to the event, such as the save the date, the invitation, the reminders, the schedule, etc.

Then, phone calls for various follow-ups and recalls follow, then the consequent updating of the list provided by the customer with the processing of the names and their outcome, as well as the subsequent sending of the confirmation vouchers with the details of the reservations.

Of course, each category (guests, speakers, sponsors, etc.) requires a different treatment.

First, you must create a list of invitees. Build the list piece by piece.

Part One

FLAG	COUNTRY	TOWN	COMPANY	REFERENT	SURNAME	NAME	PHONE AND MOBILE	E-MAIL

In "flag," you have to enter the category such as the speaker, guest, sponsor, etc.

In "country," you have to enter the name of the country of each person and in "town" the city from which the guest arrives. This will be very useful when you call.

Knowing the city and the country of the person, you need to call allows you to know what the time zone is and, therefore, to organize the recall activity according to an appropriate schedule. If you call someone at home, dawn, or at night, you may disturb and get a negative result.

In fact, the phone call must take place during working hours, possibly during a lunch break, so that you can call the person concerned without disturbing. During the call, it is good to be very precise but fast.

People do not have time and, therefore, in a few minutes, you have to give the necessary information and send back a written confirmation via email. The recall activity is, in fact, preparatory to that of sending the program and the registration, confirmation, or booking forms by e-mail.

Do not accept any verbal confirmation. Never trust what people say. They are not concentrated when they answer.

Confirmations and cancellations must only be collected in writing. This is why, in addition to the country and city from which the guest to contact comes, it is essential to have their direct email address, their landline phone, and—if possible—their mobile number.

In the next part of the list, in fact, you will see the cells relating to the email, the phone, etc., that you must fill in with the appropriate guest data.

In the "referent" text box, however, you must indicate the contact person, i.e., not necessarily the invited guest but, perhaps, the area manager of reference, etc.

The contact person is usually the one who can help you find the invited person if they do not answer by phone or email, despite your repeated contact attempts.

Part Two

TRAVEL	COST	HOTEL	TYPE OF ROOM	COST (for the night in BB)	CHECK-IN	CHECK-OUT	TOT. NIGHTS	TOTAL COST OF THE HOTEL

In the "travel" box, you must indicate whether the person travels by plane or train or with their own vehicle. You must also indicate the flight timetable, when it is issued, or the arrival and departure times of the train when you made the ticket.

In the "cost" box, you must specify the ticket price issued. This is for when you will have to make the final counts.

In the "hotel" box, you must indicate the name of the hotel assigned to that guest. In fact, not all guests can sleep in the same hotel.

So, the assignment task you make on the list is very important for the coordination with the hostesses and the welcome you will make on-site when guests arrive or leave the assigned hotel.

In the "type of room" box, you must indicate the room that the guest will occupy and, therefore, if it is a single, a double, or a double room but with single occupancy, or a triple or even a quadruple.

If a guest takes the children with them and they are small children, maybe they will need two communicating rooms.

If a guest is disabled, they will need a room adapted to their motor needs. If accompanied by a healthcare professional, the operator's room must be communicating with theirs.

If a guest is a judge under escort, the room or rooms closest to them must be assigned to the police protecting them. The allocation of the rooms also depends on the client's needs because perhaps they prefer to have a certain type of guest in a hotel or another. Or they prefer to assign higher category rooms to some major guests and standard category rooms to others.

The hotel you use for some guests, in fact, may have a category (three, four, five stars, or luxury), and this category could be higher than the one used in other hotels for other guests.

Or, in the case of a congress, where the speakers are guests, but the members are paid, you must book hotels of different categories.

The participants do not want to spend much money and, therefore, a three-star rating is more than enough. Instead, a speaker must always be hosted in a four-star, five-star, or luxury hotel.

Before choosing which hotel to accommodate your guests, whether they are speakers or participants, you must make an inspection and verify that the hotel is suitable in addition to its category.

Some hotels, for example, are four-star category only because they have a swimming pool, but their standard is that of a three-star hotel. Hosting a speaker in such a hotel is inappropriate.

When inspecting a hotel, try to check not only the best rooms the owner will want to show you but also the smaller ones.

Check if the bathroom is clean but also if it is in good condition; if the sink is not chipped if the carpet is not dirty. Even the hotel, in fact, reflects your image because you choose where to accommodate your guests, therefore—indirectly—they will also judge you based on where you made them sleep.

If some guests come from far away, notify the hotel as soon as you give them the rooming list because they may be checking in very late.

If, however, other guests need to leave later after the room's check-out time, request a late checkout. When you deliver the rooming list to the hotel, it is good to check with your hotel contact person the needs of each guest—name by name—so that there are no problems.

It is important that all details are taken into consideration not only by you but also by who will host your participants in the event and, therefore, in this case, by the hotel.

If you know that some guests will need to have lunch or dinner in the hotel, choose a hotel with an internal restaurant.

When you book a room, try to request a BB treatment, i.e., with bed and breakfast. Check if there are tourist and service taxes to be paid and agreed in advance with your customer, if these taxes are expenses that you have to pay in advance on behalf of your customer or if they are expenses that remain to be paid by the guests. Define with your client even if the guests are full credit or not. Full credit guests are those to whom you have to pay personal extras and then charge them back to your customer.

In the appropriate boxes to follow, you will have to specify all these things and always add a "notes" box in which you write details that you deem necessary, such as a customer with an allergy, etc.

At the end of the boxes listed so far, you will find the "total cost of the hotel": an essential box because inside it, you must mark the total cost of the guest's overnight stay.

In fact, there are guests who sleep one night and others who sleep two or more. Set the list in excels format so that in the appropriate cells, you can set the calculation formula.

It will be easier for you, both in the final balance and during construction, to control the costs from time to time.

Part Three

PICK-UP ARRIVAL	PICK-UP RETURN	LUNCH/DINNER	ACCOMPANYING PERSON

The third part of the list can be infinite, as it depends on what is offered to the guest and on the type of event.

I'll explain it. If the customer decides to offer pick-ups, that is, the private driver who picks up the guest at the station or airport and takes them to the hotel, the pick-up time must be written in the appropriate box as well as the name of the driver and driver's mobile phone. The same must be done for both the outward and return pick up.

If the guests attend lunch, dinner, or other activities, a box must be created for each of them and must be duly filled in. If the guest brings an accompanying person, you have to enter their name in the right box.

The list must be structured considering all the activities, movements, technical and sensitive data of the person you need to manage and who travels with them. It is essential to adequately collect all guest information and reservations. A well-made list is a fundamental tool for managing guests correctly.

The list can also be created online as well as the format of the participant form. The online tools are very effective if the type of participants use them.

If instead, they are people who do not like to register through websites or online tools, it is necessary to proceed in the traditional way, and therefore, according to the indications given so far.

Even if online tools are used, the recall activity and the adequate compilation of the list are fundamental for the correct management of the guest. After creating the list, the guest management activity provides, as mentioned above, sending the invitation by email.

The invitation can be a program, a letter of participation, a program with a registration form, etc.

In the following pages, there are several examples. Sending by email is done many times during the processing of the list, that is until confirmation or denial by the invitee has been reached. Confirmation or denial must always be received in writing. To request confirmation or denial, the recall activity is used, that is, the telephone contact about which we have already talked above.

When you have finished working on a list and then contacted all the people, it will be full of positives feedbacks (participants) or negative feedbacks (those who do not come to the event).

You keep the positive feedbacks in sheet one of your excels list, while the negative feedbacks have to be moved to sheet two. In fact, from now on, you will only work with the positives. So only with those who will come to the event. To these people, that is "the positive feedbacks" you will have to send a voucher which is a document summarizing everything they do, where and when they do it, as well as their hotel booking, their trip and—if any—their pick up when they arrive and when they leave.

Before making the voucher, obviously, you must have defined with the guest their trip and their check-in and check-out dates at the hotel.

Together with the voucher, you must also send them the plane or train ticket. That is their travel ticket.

Never issue a travel ticket unless you have written confirmation from the guest about the dates and flight/train schedules you have proposed to them.

In fact, guests often change their minds. But the tickets you issue—most of the time—are non-refundable fares and, therefore, you risk throwing a lot of money away. If, on the other hand, you have written confirmation from the guest, it is more difficult for them to change their mind.

If it does, when you have to report to your client why you had to issue two tickets for the same guest, for example, you will have their emails proving that you were not wrong, but the guest has changed their mind.

The processing of the guest management, in fact, serves to optimize expenses, i.e., to book a number of adequate rooms according to the number of people who are present, to book a number of people at lunch or dinner according to who will really be present, etc.

However—since people who sleep and eat for free are not as careful to be present as when they pay personally—having written confirmations serves to demonstrate to your client—if they ask you—that your work has been done very well, even if the guest does not show up.

It is, however, unlikely that a guest, considering the work done with the guest management, will not show up. Usually, this only happens if the guest gets sick or if there are sudden commitments.

But generally, the guest lets you know about it immediately; therefore—if you know it in time—you can cancel the reservation. In this case, if the cancellation is too close to the date of the event, surely there will be penalties to be paid that you have agreed with the hotel or airline or catering, etc. But if the cancellation occurs in good enough time, you can cancel without paying any penalty.

Getting guests used to sending written confirmations and sending written cancellations is the result of good guest management.

And it is very useful for optimizing costs and having a full but not overflowing room, for having a dinner with all the tables occupied without empty seats, for not having too many people who use private transfer compared to the seats onboard, etc.

Guest management is the activity that ensures the success of the event and therefore requires a lot of attention.

It is the added value that, together with convention management, makes a complete and truly professional event organizer. The difference, in fact, between a person who organizes events and an event manager is determined by a mix between convention and guest management.

They are two different, but equally important skills to create a successful event.

Let's see, for example, the different types of letters that can be sent according to the different types of guests and the different situations to manage.

CHAPTER 7:

THE SPEAKERS AND/OR THE GUESTS

Here are four examples necessary for this type of management:

1. Invitation Letter

The invitation letter is the one that serves to describe the program of the event to the invitee, and that must include all the details. It can be signed by the president of the congress or—in the case of a corporate event—by the commercial director, etc.

Inside it, however, all the references of the organizational secretariat must be present, regardless of whether it is signed by the customer or not.

The invitation letter, in fact, is the first working tool of the guest management and is the one that introduces the organizational secretariat.

The invitation letter not only introduces the organizational secretariat but "authorizes" it in the truest sense of the word to contact the guests on behalf of the client company or on behalf of the company that organizes the scientific or political event.

2. Hospitality Form

The registration or hospitality form that the invitee must fill in and send back by email to the organizational secretariat may or may not be joined to the invitation letter.

The hospitality form or even the registration form, in the case of a member who registers their presence at a congress, may vary in the format as in the indications given depending on the type of event.

But the structure, in general, is very similar to all these types of forms.

3. Welcome Letter

The welcome letter is a letter that is usually found in the hotel room, and that welcomes guests and summarizes—again—all that was written in the voucher: the meeting points, the activities, the places where they take place, the times they take place, etc.

No travel ticket must be attached to the welcome letter: the guest has now arrived, so their travel tickets have been received and used.

Together with the welcome letter, a gift can be found in the guest room. In this case, you must add a "with compliments" note.

4. Voucher

The voucher is preparatory to the welcome letter and is a sort of "vademecum" for the invitee. But since most guests lose the voucher, or forget it, and don't remember where to go and what to do, the welcome letter serves just as an "additional voucher."

The difference between the actual voucher and the welcome letter is that travel tickets must also be attached to the voucher.

A well-made voucher is short but does not leave out any important details. It is colorful, that is, with images of the venue or hotel or location where the event takes place and the logo of the customer.

It must always be sent in PDF format as it is a closed document that is not subject to modification. The voucher must therefore be useful, but also beautiful.

If a specific graphic image is created for the event, the voucher will have this graphic image, but it must also be enriched with images or frames or other forms of graphic decorations that can be easily created digitally.

That is, it is a work tool, and therefore, it must not be sent by a graphic designer as if it were a printout. But this does not mean that its presentation should be that of an insignificant email.

A middle ground between the two. The voucher must always be double checked between two staff members. One person reads the list (on whose information the voucher is produced), and the other checks the voucher.

This double-check allows you to make sure that there are no mistakes, that the information contained in the list is the same as that written in the voucher, but—above all—allows you to check that you have not forgotten anything.

That is, it is not just a summary for your guest but an additional check for you that verifies that you have not missed any details.

Example—Invitation Letter

Name of the event

Date

Place

To the kind attention of

Dear Dr. _____,

I am writing to you in my capacity as planner and organizer of the above-mentioned Meeting, and I am enclosing herewith the conference program **with the latest changes introduced thereto, as per indications from the Scientific Board of the Meeting**.

For your podium presentation, we can make arrangements for a twin slide projection, overhead projector, a connection for projections from your own computer, and standard VHS projection, as needed.

Please inform us by means of the enclosed form if you plan to use any of the above technical resources so that we can make them appropriately available to you.

I am also informing you that on ____ (month, date) next, at 8.30 p.m., a **Welcome** _____ will be hosted by Prof. _____ in _____ (address _____), where you are kindly expected as distinguished guest.

I would appreciate it if **by** _____ (*month, date*) next you can complete the enclosed form and thereby notify us of your requirements concerning your podium presentation and your stay at _____ town during the days of the Meeting. In this respect, a room will be available for you at the **Hotel** _____, located in _____.

Our Secretariat is ready to assist you with the arrangements for your travel to our city, and for such purpose, please refer again to the enclosed form. In this respect, I am informing you that we shall cover all travel expenses only for yourself.

Should you wish to travel in the company of another person, we can take care of an additional seat reservation and notify you of the deadline by which you can purchase the airplane ticket for the person accompanying you.

However, should you prefer to organize your travel by yourself, your airplane fare will be reimbursed to you upon presentation of the original ticket to our Secretariat after the meeting.

I wish to point out that the airplane ticket provided by us will be a closed ticket with fixed dates and times; therefore, please see to it that any changes are avoided or limited as much as possible.

Please do not hesitate to contact me for any additional information. I remain, with compliments,

Yours Sincerely

Attachments: scientific program; hospitality form.

Example—Hospitality Form

Name of the event

Date

Place

To the kind attention of

Day ___ Month ___ Year ___

Name _____

Family name _____

For my presentation, I shall use:

❏ Standard VHS videotape

❏ Twin slide projection

❏ Overhead projector

❏ Computer projection

I hereby confirm my presence:

At the soirée of ____ (month, date), ___ (year):

YES ☐   NO ☐

With accompanying person:

YES ☐   NO ☐

I hereby confirm my hotel reservation:

❏ Single room

❏ Double room

Check-in date   _____

Check-out date   _____

Total No. of nights   _____

Please organize my transfer by:

☐   Airplane

☐   Train

☐   I do not need any travel arrangements

For any further information or notification please contact: _____

Example—Welcome Letter

Name of the event

Date

Place

To the kind attention of

Day ___ Month ___ Year ___

___ hr. Meeting point in the hotel hall and departure by bus to _____.

___ hr. **Welcome coffee** and registration of the participants at the reception.

___ hr. Technical presentations.

Follow Hands-on demonstrations.

___ hr. **Lunch Break.**

___ hr. Technical presentations.

Follow Hands-on demonstrations.

___ hr. End of presentations and demonstrations and departure by bus to the hotel.

___ hr. Meeting point in the hall of the hotel.

Departure by bus to _____.

___ hr. Return to the hotel by bus.

Day ___ Month ___ Year ___

Check-out before ___ hr. and individual departures.

For any further information, our Organizational Staff is at your disposal at the following telephone numbers: _____

Yours sincerely,

Example—Voucher

Name of the event

Date

Place

To the kind attention of

VOUCHER

We are glad to confirm the following reservations:

N° 1 room at:

HOTEL _____

Address _____

Town _____

(ph. + _____)

Check-in date: ____

Check-out date: ____

Total n. of nights: ____

Month _____ Date _____ (for instance, October 5th, year _____)— _____ p.m./a.m.

Welcome Dinner *(or what is)*

Restaurant _____. Address _____, _____ - _____

Phone __ ___ - ___

_____ p.m.: **Welcome Cocktail**

Venue _____, Palace _____

_____ p.m.: **Concert** _____. Location "_____"

Venue _____, palace _____

I remind you that your flight fare will be refunded to you upon presentation of the original ticket to our Secretariat after the meeting.

Looking forward to seeing you in _____ *(or what is)*,

Yours Sincerely,

CHAPTER 8:

THE ABSTRACT

Here are two examples necessary to this type of management:

1. Request Letter

The letter requesting an abstract has scientific content, which is agreed with the scientific company that organizes the congress.

The abstract is, in fact, present only in scientific conferences, i.e., medical or technical conferences or those in the sector.

So, an event such as a concert, for example, does not provide for this type of request or for the management of people, often doctors, who must present a summary of their scientific work at the congress.

Obviously, there are many types of events, and therefore, also the types of documents that must be produced depending on what type of event it is.

Usually, during a medical congress, the scientific commission—after judging the abstracts received—selects the best ones that are published in the volume of the documents or in a special book that is the volume of the abstracts. Others can be hung as posters or projected in the classroom.

The use and the tool according to which the abstract will be presented does not depend on the participant but the scientific committee that judges and chooses it.

2. Confirmation Letter

The confirmation letter of the abstract selected and chosen by the scientific committee will explain how it will be presented, that is, whether as a poster, as a text, as a lecture, etc.

In the letter, there will also be all the details on the size of the poster, as well as the length of the text in case of publication, and the verbal length in case of oral presentation.

Because this section could have infinite examples which, however, are all closely related to the type of event and, therefore, only one explanatory model is enough.

The section of an event dedicated to abstracts usually allows young professionals to get noticed. They have the opportunity to show their work to a selected and very large audience: the event is a very important opportunity for them.

In fact, both the abstracts that are exposed and those that are published are positive and often very valid references in the work curriculum of the young professional.

At the end of an event, especially if scientific or technical or commercial, a publication is often made, which is precisely the

"Volume of the Proceedings" (i.e., all that was said or presented during the event).

It is possible that two publications may also be produced: the volume of abstracts and the volume of documents.

In the case of corporate events, there are no scientific publications of this kind, but if a volume is made, it is usually with the souvenir photos of the event or linked to the products of the company that organizes it.

The final product is of another kind and value. Not scientific but commercial.

A book of the event is, in fact, a memory to be sent to customers or to the agents who participated, but it is also a production that conveys—sometimes—the company's products. It, therefore, has a double commercial and marketing value.

But even in this case, an immense chapter of examples could be opened because, depending on the type of event and the target to which it refers, the eventual final publication has a greater or lesser value.

Example—Request Letter

Name of the event

Date

Place

To the kind attention of

Subject:

POSTER SESSION: _____ National Conference on _____

Place _____, venue _____, date month year _____

Dear Doctors,

With reference to the Conference on the subject and on behalf of the President and Scientific Council, I will contact you to define the logistic aspects of the posters' bill-posting; it must have dimension 70 cm (base) x100 cm (height).

Each author, charged with the bill-posting of their poster (single or collective), have to apply to the reception of the Conference before the beginning of works to receive the necessary material: ribbon, etc.

Each poster is marked by a number (LOOK AT THE ATTACHMENT) fixed on the windows destined for the poster session: the author charged with the bill-posting, therefore, have to collocate their poster on the window marked by the corresponding number.

Best Regards,

Poster Session

1. **Example of title** _____

2. **Example of title** _____

Etc.

Example—Confirmation Letter

Name of the event

Date

Place

To the kind attention of

Subject: Abstract acceptance sent in the occasion of _____ National Congress of _____.

City _____, congress venue _____, date _____ month _____ year _____

Dear _____,

With reference to the Conference on the subject and to the names of the President and Scientific Council, I would like to communicate to you the acceptance of the following productions:

TITLE

_____

They will be presented as a predefined intervention of _____ minutes (discussion ___) on _____, at _____ and at _____.

TITLE

_____

It will be presented as a free speech of _____ minutes (discussion ___) on _____, at _____.

CHAPTER 9:

THE SPONSOR

Sponsors are among the most important subjects of an event not only because they contribute to covering costs, but because—if they are satisfied with the event—they are pleased to sponsor others. Therefore, their satisfaction implies the possibility of indirect business continuity also for the agency that organizes the event.

The relationship with the sponsors is very stimulating because their participation in the event is of many types. It can be in the form of branding of the printed matter/a trademark on the printed materials, i.e., the affixing of their logo on them. Or it can also extend to the personalization of signs and any other form of advertising, such as posters, newspapers, videos, etc.

In some cases, they may decide to organize an event within the event.

This event can be scientific (such as a satellite symposium) or social (for example, the sponsorship of the gala dinner and, therefore, the whole evening will be branded). This means that the sponsor will have its logo everywhere, from gifts to centerpieces to posters to everything that happens during the evening.

Furthermore, some sponsors also decide to be present in the venue where the event takes place with a stand and, therefore, with an exhibition of their products.

The relationship with the sponsors thus allows you to see all the commercial and marketing possibilities that companies usually use and which are: stands at sector fairs, publications, advertising, etc.

All these different opportunities are to be offered to companies that may be interested in participating in an event in terms of sponsors. A contract will then be drawn up with each one, which, based on the agreed amount, will establish the type of participation of the adhering sponsor.

The first invitation letter that is sent to a sponsor company is, in fact, a letter in which the initiative is presented and which lists all the possibilities for participation and the cost.

Any form of participation or, in this case, sponsorship implies a disbursement of money by the sponsoring company.

The fee relating to the type of participation that is chosen is defined by the agency that organizes the event together with the customer or the company that promotes it. It is higher or lower, depending on participation.

For example, if a sponsor company decides to participate only by placing its logo on the printed matter, it will pay a certain amount. But if instead, they decide to participate with many forms of sponsorship, the amount they will pay will be the sum of all the opportunities chosen.

There are cases in which, however, the sponsor pays a very high figure, which includes not only all the forms of sponsorship envisaged but goes much further. In this case, we speak of the main sponsorship.

The main sponsor is the company or institution that has a primary interest in the sector of reference for the event and, therefore, has a greater interest in being there.

The processing of the sponsors is very delicate because it is like organizing many small events for many companies altogether.

The collection of the sums paid by the sponsors to the agency must be reported at the end of the event, as well as that deriving from registration fees and/or any other paying institution.

The agency is, therefore, the administrative driving force of an event, as well as the operational and creative one. Its role is very important because it manages the money of all the subjects involved both as income and as outputs.

There are three types of letters used in the management of sponsors:

- Proposal letter
- Possibility of promotional intervention
- Letter of thanks at the end of the event

The **first** concerns the introduction of the initiative.

The **second** concerns the proposals.

The **third** is sent at the end of the event and is a "thank you letter." In some cases, the list of participants may also be attached to it. It depends on whether the sponsor requests it and whether the privacy laws allow it.

The three letters—of which below are the three basic models—are obviously only a work tool which, however, has no value if it is not supported by an intense telephone recall activity and then by a large, indeed very large commercial capacity.

To close a contract with a sponsor, attitude is more important than competence. And in addition to attitude, you need the right contacts. For example, many sponsors are reported directly by the customer that organizes the event or, in the case of a medical event, by the president of the congress.

In the latter case, these are companies linked to the doctor, institution, or hospital that promotes the event because they are suppliers of products that the hospital (for example) buys during the year.

For instance, the operating unit of a hospital that buys respirators, wheelchairs, prostheses, etc. There may be sport or cultural events sponsored by companies that apparently—have no interest strictly related to the subject of the event.

But in this case, visibility at an important concert or a football game is essential to advertise your product.

The world of sponsorships is complex and very vast. Again, one type of sponsorship or another, one type of company or another, depends on the event and the target to which the event refers.

Once the sponsor proposal has been sent, and once the contract with the company that sponsors the event or with the companies that sponsor the event has been closed, the exhibitor regulation must be drawn up.

This is a very important document that must be drawn up considering all the agreements with the venue where the event takes place, because—based on them—the exhibiting presence of the companies will be regulated.

So, if they can hang things on the walls, what kind of stands they can make, how big the stand can be, where it can be placed, etc., the location of a stand in a transit area is obviously more advantageous than the company exhibiting in an area with little access to the public.

The area in which to make the stand that has better visibility must be sold at a higher price than the stand that is positioned in a less visible place.

The size of the stand also affects. If a sponsor company buys a small space, it will pay less than a company that buys a huge space. Just like at the fair: the largest stand occupies a larger exhibition area and costs more. It is not only a cost linked to the actual setting, that is, to the walls, the table, the chairs, but it is a cost determined by the greater or lesser space that is occupied.

For the same space occupied, the sponsor who exhibits in the area close to the catering service has greater visibility than the sponsor who exhibits in the entrance hall, for example. The selling price of the space is, therefore, also determined by this. Size and visibility are both important.

All this must be detailed in the exhibitor regulation, which is a real contract that must be signed by the sponsor company. Furthermore, the exhibitor regulation safeguards the agency in case the sponsor posts posters, pierces the wall, or has behaviors not authorized by the venue. In the event of a dispute, in fact, the office may take recourse to the sponsor company directly.

If, however, there is no signed exhibitor regulation, all responsibility rests with the agency that organizes the event.

The exhibitors regulation also includes detailed items such as the cost of porters (which—if is required—is a separate expense to be paid by the sponsor), the cost of storing goods if they arrive too many days before the event and if they are not collected at the end of the event, etc.

That is, every logistical, operational, and commercial situation must be detailed clearly and with extreme precision in the exhibitor regulation to protect all parties involved.

For example: If in the sponsorship provided by the company it is foreseen—by contract and by the exhibitor's regulation—that the stand will be given to them pre-set up, therefore, with tables and chairs as well as walls, the agency must do so.

If, on the other hand, the company buys only one exhibition space but is free to set it up as it thinks, with its material, the agency will have to make sure that this material is suitable for the current regulations (as indicated in the regulation for exhibitors), both for fire and other rules.

There is no model of exhibitor regulation, as it depends on the venue in which the event takes place.

For instance, if an event takes place on the track and is an event dedicated to motorcycles or cars, the exhibitor regulation must consider the need for sports activities that require the mandatory presence of doctors, ambulances, etc.

In track events, for example, the same guests, therefore, not only the sponsor companies, if they want to ride a high-speed motorcycle on the circuit, must first pass a medical examination that guarantees that they do not have high blood pressure and that they do not have heart disease. The adrenaline produced by speed could, in fact, cause a heart attack.

Everyone then must sign a declaration of release that is a release of responsibility if something happens. But this declaration, without the track doctor's certificate, attesting the state of full and good health, has no value.

Similarly, sponsors exhibiting in places like these must comply with regulations other than those exhibiting in a conference venue.

There are no easier venues than others in relation to exhibitor regulations: each has its own peculiarities and critical issues. But some locations certainly have more risky issues than others.

At a track event—for example—the participation of the sponsor can also materialize with the organization of competitions within the event itself or of wedding activities, perhaps on motorcycles or production machines of the sponsor company.

If it is a question of very large events, in particular, those open to the public, the regulation of the activities to be offered to the participants (whether they are organized directly by the agency or directly implemented by the sponsors with their staff) must be made with extreme precision. The larger the number of people, the greater the risks. This is the reason because all this must be regulated in the abovementioned exhibitor regulation and in the sponsorship contract, which provides in detail the type of activity, the car or motorbike that will be used, the duration, the level of danger, etc. Sponsor management is, therefore, a very complex part of an event and requires a person to oversee the overall job. But—if the event is big and there are many sponsors—one person is not enough. Having said that, I would say that we can evaluate the examples of letters to follow, but—I repeat—taking into account that they are only traces of work, that is, drafts of what can be negotiated with a sponsor.

The letters that follow are—so to speak—a starting point and, at the same time, a reference model.

Example—Proposal Letter

Name of the event

Date

Place

To the kind attention of

Dear Dr. _____,

I want to inform you that on _____ will be proposed at _____, the _____ National Conference on _____.

The Congress venue will be _____.

It is provided that at the Conference will participate in the most important keynote of that sector, with an estimated presence of about _____ among participants and accompanying persons. The Institutional Importance of the Conference—that will occur under the patronage of _____—is evidenced not only by the presence of _____ but also by that of some important members of the National Government and Parliament.

Owing to the importance of the Conference and the promotional opportunity which represents an excellent trademark like yours, I think that you could not miss it. I send you herewith enclosed proof of the program of the Conference and a prospect of the general opportunities of participation. Whether the enterprise is of your interest, it will be a pleasure for us to meet each other and discuss the _____.

I will remain at your disposal for any clarification.

Best Regards,

For the Organizing Secretariat.

Example—Possibility of Promotional Intervention

Name of the event

Date

Place

To the kind attention of

Since _____ are became the most important and appreciated meeting for all sector's operators of our country and at the international level, here follow some proposals of lecture for _companies_ which have the pleasure to present their products and/or to underline their role in this sector.

Description

1. Acquisition of expositive spaces
2. Acquisition of advertising spaces on wall posters
3. Personalization of congress materials
4. Personalization of congress events
5. Organization of satellite symposiums
6. Branded relations
7. Distribution of congress gifts
8. Main sponsorship

Pay attention: Investments to € ____ give a free entrance, higher investments give an extra free entrance for each € ____ of expense.

- **Acquisition of expositive spaces**

In the area _____ located _____ are prepared no. _____ stands, available separated or linked together.

It is possible to find enclosed the plant of spaces in order to choose those, which in case fits best.

Each stand will have _____ made up of _____ with _____.

Quotation for each stand no. _____ (attention: different position = different cost) € _____.

- **Acquisition of advertising spaces on wall posters**

The following possibilities are available:

Second, third, or fourth of cover

Or _____, etc.

- **Points 3–8 above mentioned depending on the type of the event.**

Example—Letter of Thanks at the End of the Event

Name of the event

Date

Place

To the kind attention of

Dear _____,

I am writing with reference to the _____, that has taken place at _____ on _____.

On behalf of _____, I would like to thank you and the Company you represent very much for having contributed in such a great way to the perfect realization of the Meeting.

Indeed, the presence of _____ registered participants, I enclose herewith the list, is proof of the strong interest provoked by this enterprise.

(N.B.: *You can attach the list only if the privacy is ok, etc.*)

Hoping you are satisfied with the work done, I hope we will work together in the next future.

Best Regards,

For the Organizing Secretariat.

CONCLUSION

And here we are at the end of the book.

By dedicating a day to each of the individual sections listed here, in a week—or rather, in just five days—you will have acquired all the tools of the trade to be an event organizer. However, it is essential to practice them. And most of all, practice with someone who has been doing this job for some time and who can give you the opportunity to learn on the field. Nothing is more instructive than a live event.

Only by finding yourself in the midst of difficulties and satisfactions, you will be able to understand if this job is for you, if you think you can love it and if you are able to withstand the pressures that this activity entails.

It is a unique and exciting job. It is never equal to itself. Impossible to get bored. But, if you want to become an event manager, you must always aim for the best.

Anyone can organize an event, but this does not mean that they are an event manager.

The difference is in the quality, in the level of perfection, in the attention to detail, in the creativity with which each event is the event, the unique, special one, designed and created especially for that customer.

A shirt is always a shirt, but if it is cut and sewn by a stylist, it falls on you completely differently than a shirt bought at the market. With this book, you can do any type of event because you have all the necessary tools.

But if your "shirt" will be that of a stylist or that of a market stall, this will be decided by your desire to be an event manager.

At the End of Any Event...

Do not forget to thank your staff, your client, your suppliers, not only sponsors (if any), and volunteers (if any).

- Finalize the balance as quickly as possible.
- Post the photos on your website.

ABOUT THE AUTHOR

Daniela Liccardo is born in Naples in 1968, and—since she was a girl—she stands out for her desire to organize.

She begins with the organization of the annual school play at the elementary school, up to the political activity when in high superior school, she is one of the representatives of the Institute until the university period, which marks the first step towards the world of organization of events.

During her university years, in fact, Daniela collaborates in the organization of the press offices for Giulio Einaudi Editore, the most prestigious Italian publishing house.

She collaborates at the organization of the launches of the books, rather than the presentations of the new authors (Giulio Einaudi is an incredible talent scout) up to the open house of the various local offices of the Italian publishing house.

The meeting with Giulio Einaudi, the founder of the publishing house that takes its name, is crucial for Daniela's professional growth path, who learns the importance of doing everything with excellence.

The cultural climate in Giulio Einaudi Editore is stimulating. It allows Daniela to get in touch with various editorial realities such as some art magazines, for which she begins to write, publishing articles on exhibitions of modern and contemporary art, which are her great passion.

But soon, Daniela goes directly from the articles to the organization of the exhibitions for the art galleries and then also for the National Gallery (Pinacoteca) and the Institution for Historical and Artistic Heritage.

In the meantime, she graduates with honors from the University of Bologna and begins her post-graduate internship at the Pecci Museum, the most important Museum of Contemporary Art in Italy.

And it is precisely during the internship in Pecci that Daniela gets in touch with Andrea Emiliani, awarded with countless international prizes for museography.

He takes Daniela under his protective wing and opens the doors to her in a new and exciting world: the organization of museum services.

Daniela begins to collaborate with the company that organizes the major international exhibitions for the National Gallery (Pinacoteca), but not only the exhibitions: also the bookshop, merchandising, concerts, conferences. She discovers the liveliness of the event and falls in love with its exciting speed: the event opens and closes within a few days, in which it offers incredibly stimulating moments to all those who took part, be they the creators or the participants.

And, on the occasion of a conference that Daniela organizes in the Pinacoteca, takes place the meeting that determines the professional turning point in her life. She meets the owner of one of the most important Italian congress agencies.

Daniela begins working on the organization of medical, political, accountant, notary, and industrial congresses. They are very rich years, during which a lot of money spins and wonderful events can be realized, with fabulous settings and incredible social programs: a dream!

As responsible, Daniela coordinates and supervises the work of her other colleagues, starting from the one who takes care of the registration fee to the one who is dedicated to the suppliers, up to those who take care of the management of the speakers and guests.

Daniela directly processes the relationship with the customer and the management of the sponsors. And it is precisely the direct relationship with the companies (in the congress agency only sponsor of the event) that becomes the core business of the agency that Daniela founds and which she still owns.

The sponsors participating in the conferences have both an exhibition collaboration (the stand) and a scientific collaboration (the symposium or the meeting or a lecture within the congress).

Daniela has the opportunity to deal with all corporate organizational services at 360 degrees and discovers that this—among all the types of organizations she has done in her life—is the one she likes best, and that gives her the greatest satisfaction.

Daniela's agency, in fact, organizes all types of corporate events in Italy and abroad, from the fair to the incentive trip, from the open house to the meeting for agents or customers, from the family day to the gala dinner, etc.

Printed in Great Britain
by Amazon